Davidson Family Tree

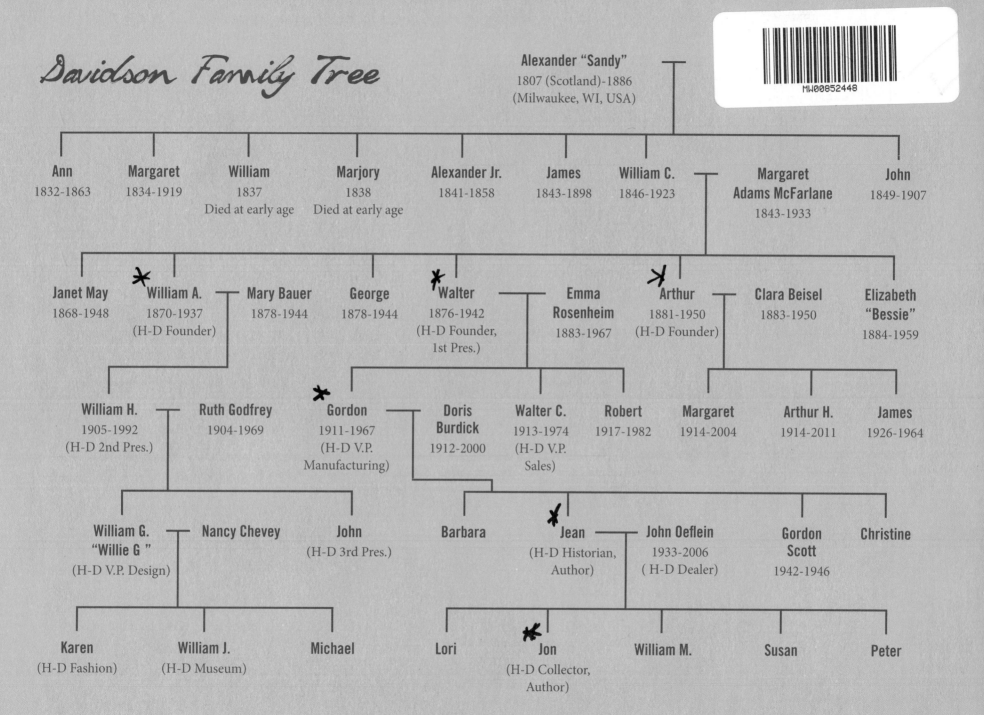

Alexander "Sandy"
1807 (Scotland)-1886
(Milwaukee, WI, USA)

Ann
1832-1863

Margaret
1834-1919

William
1837
Died at early age

Marjory
1838
Died at early age

Alexander Jr.
1841-1858

James
1843-1898

William C.
1846-1923

Margaret
Adams McFarlane
1843-1933

John
1849-1907

Janet May
1868-1948

William A.
1870-1937
(H-D Founder)

Mary Bauer
1878-1944

George
1878-1944

Walter
1876-1942
(H-D Founder,
1st Pres.)

Emma
Rosenheim
1883-1967

Arthur
1881-1950
(H-D Founder)

Clara Beisel
1883-1950

Elizabeth
"Bessie"
1884-1959

William H.
1905-1992
(H-D 2nd Pres.)

Ruth Godfrey
1904-1969

Gordon
1911-1967
(H-D V.P.
Manufacturing)

Doris
Burdick
1912-2000

Walter C.
1913-1974
(H-D V.P.
Sales)

Robert
1917-1982

Margaret
1914-2004

Arthur H.
1914-2011

James
1926-1964

William G.
"Willie G"
(H-D V.P. Design)

Nancy Chevey

John
(H-D 3rd Pres.)

Barbara

Jean
(H-D Historian,
Author)

John Oeflein
1933-2006
(H-D Dealer)

Gordon
Scott
1942-1946

Christine

Karen
(H-D Fashion)

William J.
(H-D Museum)

Michael

Lori

Jon
(H-D Collector,
Author)

William M.

Susan

Peter

Unfortunately, this family tree does not show all the family members.

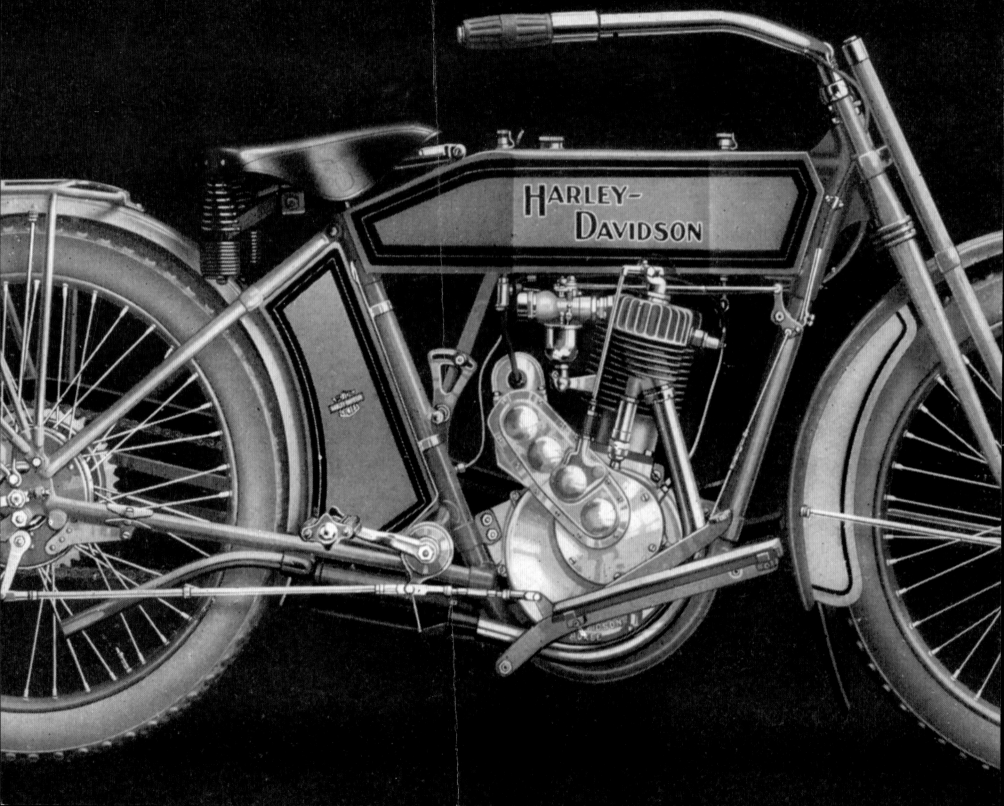

HARLEY-DAVIDSON FAMILY MEMORIES

By JEAN DAVIDSON and JON DAVIDSON OEFLEIN

Octane Press, Edition 1.0, October 2013

ISBN: 1937747182
ISBN-13: 978-1-937747-18-3

Proofread by Leah Noel and Steve Peters
Design by Diana Boger
Printed in China

DEDICATION

I would like to dedicate this book to my late father John H. Oeflein. First, for his rebellious nature that attracted my mother and led to the start of my wonderful life. Second, for his love of antique motorcycles that he passed on to me, and especially for his ever-present love and support. I miss him every day.　　　　　　　　　—Jon Davidson Oeflein

I would like to dedicate this book to all the fans of Harley-Davidson motorcycles. It is my pleasure to share my family history with people all over the world. It makes me smile every time I see the family name on a motorcycle.
　　　　　　　　　　　　　　—Jean Davidson

ACKNOWLEDGMENTS

Jon and Jean would like to thank the following people for contributing photographs, information and/or stories: Barbara Baumann, William Oeflein, Peter Oeflein, Nicolas Davidson Oeflein, Lori Walker, Susan Davidson Lee, Richard Marshall Jr., Roger Klopfenstein, the late Arthur Davidson, Al Wasserman, Jim Wallace, Bob Jameson, the late Liz Moyle, Jim and Kathy Bruce, Tim Talleur, Mary Harley Stocking, the late Sarah Harley, John Harley, Heather McDonell, Anthony Jankoski, Ray Wolf, Jerry Zielinski, John Clark, Mary O'Connor, E. J. Kuhn, Steve Peters, Nancy Greifenhagen, Kimberly Thomas, Bill Jackson, and the Harley-Davidson Motor Company Archives.

CONTENTS

Introduction 1

1 Catching a Dream 2

2 Building the Family Business 16

3 Storied Careers 31

4 Following Father 47

5 Scotland 67

6 The Lakes 74

7 Family Weddings 86

8 Family Dealership 92

9 Raised on Two Wheels 103

10 Evel 116

11 Fun and Games 123

12 Racing 130

13 Up and Over the Top 140

14 The Law 144

15 On the Lighter Side 151

16 Celebrate Harley-Davidson 154

Index 168

INTRODUCTION

I find it so amazing that among the many companies that tried their hand at making motorcycles in the early 1900s, Harley-Davidson is the only one that survived. I am so proud to be the great-grandson of Walter Davidson, one of the founders and first president of the Harley-Davidson Motor Co. I wish I could have met him. Despite his stoic, serious public and business persona, he was quite different in private life. He was known to love holding and playing with his children and grandchildren. I am sure if we would have lived in the same era we would have spent some great times together.

I am also proud of my grandfather, Gordon Davidson. I wish his life would not have been cut so short by the still mysterious monster called cancer. I have great memories of him that I will always hold in my mind.

But perhaps I am most proud of my own father, John H. Oeflein, who after marrying my mother, Jean Davidson, spent years in the trenches of the motorcycle business operating a successful H-D dealership that represented Milwaukee, the birthplace of the brand. He also was the person who coaxed me into taking one of his antique motorcycles for a ride on a warm evening many summers ago. The bike was a 1940 Harley-Davidson EL with the legendary 61-cubic-inch OHV (Knucklehead) motor. He said I should take it easy for a few miles since she hadn't been ridden in a while. He then said, "Why don't you take her around Big Cedar Lake and then let me know what you think about the old bikes when you get back?" I did just that and the hook was set. I could feel my ancestors with me on that ride, and it got me thinking about my family history, and in a way led to this book.

I recently stopped by my local library and saw an entire shelf of books on the Harley-Davidson Motor Co. Two of these books were written by my own dear mother, who is truly doing her part to keep our family history alive. I then left and walked a block to my bike and saw three different people wearing H-D T-shirts and a dog wearing a H-D collar. I proceeded to jump on my Davidson (my grandmother, Doris Davidson, didn't like it when people abbreviated the name the other way) and on my short ride home I was passed by five different H-D riders, and they all gave me the wave (a low, open hand jesture flashed between fellow H-D riders). William, Walter, and Arthur Davidson, along with William Harley, did indeed start something magical, and it is still very much alive today.

Jon Davidson Oeflein
December 2012

CHAPTER 1

CATCHING a DREAM

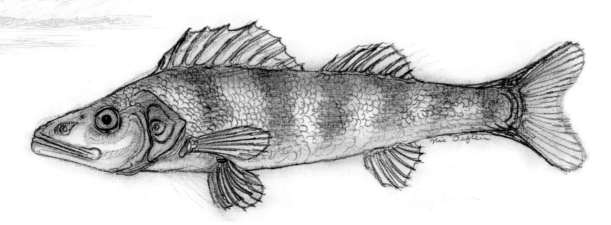

"My grandfather, Walter Davidson, was a boy with a lot of energy. He was always experimenting with new ideas and was fascinated by how things worked. He would spend hours taking things apart and then putting them back together again. He bought his first bicycle in 1893 for $35. The family story is that Walter would drive everyone crazy with his obsession of keeping his bicycle in perfect condition. He would spend hours taking it apart and putting it back together on the kitchen table!" ❁ JD

"The iconic Harley-Davidson Motor Company had a humble beginning. Arthur Davidson and William S. Harley were neighbors and best buddies. They lived in Milwaukee, WI, Arthur on Ninth Street, and William right around the corner on Clybourn. Their main interest in their spare time was fishing. The problem was the lakes they enjoyed were some 30 miles away. This was a long pedal on their bikes and started their dream of having a motorized bicycle." ▣ JDO

"Fortunately for our young inventors, Arthur's dad and two of his brothers, Walter and William, worked building trains for the railroad. This proved to be a great resource for them as they pursued building their machine. The railroad shops had all the tools and equipment they needed to make any part they could dream up. Some say the first H-D prototypes were actually built in the Milwaukee Road train shop!" ❁ JD

"My great-grandfather loved to ride his bicycle. One time he wanted to see how fast he could ride the almost 80 miles to Madison, WI, and then back home. He did it in ten hours and that was over dirt roads on a one-speed bike! The next day he was so sore that he couldn't even sit up and had to recoup for a couple of days lying in bed." ☐ JDO

"When my grandfather, Walter, was only 13 years old, he became fascinated by electricity. He made a workshop in their basement and taught himself the process of electroplating. He started taking small metal things from around the house and changing their outer coating from copper to nickel or silver. Everyone had to start hiding their personal items out of fear they would be taken to the basement!" ✳ JD

"My great-grandfather then became fascinated with the street cars that went past their house and this led him to start experimenting with electricity. He even developed his own storage batteries. He became an electrician at a young age and used these skills while employed at several Milwaukee companies." ☐ JDO

"Arthur Davidson was smaller in stature, but huge in personality. He downright loved people and was a natural communicator with a quick wit and the gift of gab. His son Arthur Harley Davidson told me about his dad's fondness of a good joke. He could tell them and also loved to hear them. He had a way of putting people at ease with a handshake and a good old slap on the back." ▦ JDO

"Arthur Davidson was good friends with Ole Evinrude. Ole didn't need to make a motor bike to get to the lake, because he already lived on Lake Ripley, in Cambridge, WI. What he did need was a way to get across the lake to see a girl he had a fancy for. Rowing was the only option until he started making the famous Evinrude outboard motors. Some say he wanted the motor to get an ice cream cone across the lake to his girl before it melted. However, one of his relatives told me that he just didn't want to be too tired from all that rowing when he finally got across the lake to his girlfriend." ✸ JD

Arthur Davidson was working as a pattern maker around the turn of the century at Pawling and Harnischfeger Co. He is at the bottom of the wheel. Above him is Ole Evinrude.

"Before Harnischfeger, William Harley worked at the Meiselbach Manufacturing Company. They produced bicycles that were all the rage at this time. It was a new mode of transportation as well as recreation. Many companies had sprung up to meet this new demand." JDO

William S. Harley is seen sitting on the stool in front. He was working as a draftsman at Pawling and Harnischfeger Co. in 1901.

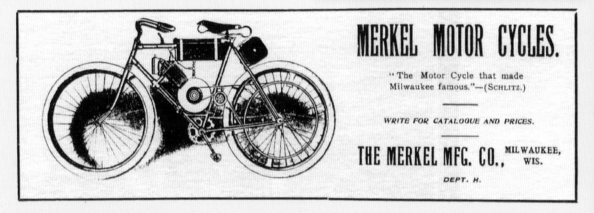

"One warm summer evening, Arthur and William Harley went to see performer Anna Held, who was the talk of the town. She was a French voluptuous beauty who did a vaudeville stage performance. At the end of the show she rode an early motor bike across the stage. The boys were awestruck by the woman's curvy body, and also loved the machine." ❋ JD

"Perhaps seeing Anna Held that night further motivated the boys to try to build their own motorcycle, or maybe it was seeing motorcycles start to appear on the streets of their town. Two outfits were already building motorcycles in Wisconsin. The Mitchell was being produced in Racine and the Merkel right in Milwaukee! There were even motorcycles being produced on the East Coast that had made their way to Milwaukee, namely the Indian, which turned out to be Harley's biggest rival for years to come." ▨ JDO

**Performer/Actress
Anna Held in 1906.**

Young Walter Davidson (second from left) finishes a day of hard work at the railroad yard, Parsons, KS, in 1902.

"The problem that Arthur and William had with their early motor bike experiment was they needed a good mechanic. In 1903, my grandfather, Walter, was working as a machinist for the Katy Railroad in Parsons, KS. He was also a skilled mechanic and electrician. He was just what his younger brother, Arthur, needed to make their motorcycle dreams come true." ✳ JD

"Lucky for everyone, Walter was coming home for his older brother William's wedding. Along with the wedding invitation that Walter received was a small note from Arthur promising him a ride on their new motor bike.

When Walter got home for the wedding in April of 1903, much to his dismay the bike project was still in many pieces on the basement floor. When he complained about not being able to go for a ride, Arthur told him he could ride it, as soon as he put it together!" ▣ JDO

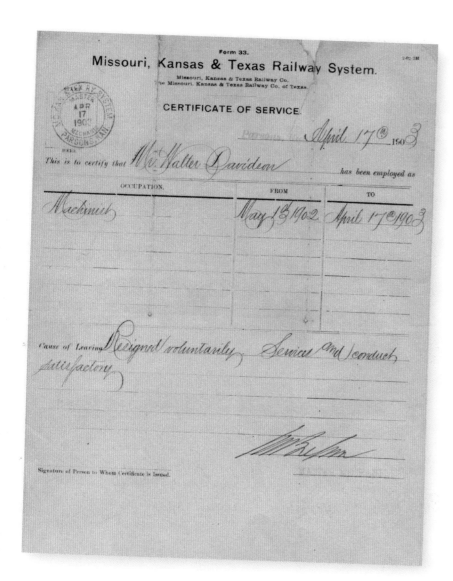

LEFT: Walter Davidson in 1903.

OPPOSITE: The railroad shops in Parsons, KS. The new locomotives can be seen lined up on the left.

BELOW: The exterior of the beautiful Missouri, Kansas and Texas Railroad Depot in Parsons, KS. The railroad was known to many as the Katy.

M. K. & T. Depot, Parsons, Kansas.

"The entire Davidson family was involved with the making of Harley-Davidsons. The founder's father built homes for the employees. The founder's sister, Bessie, kept the financial books in order. The older sister, Janet, hand-painted the details on the early bikes. When the young founders had all their money stolen, the uncle, James McLay, came to their rescue by giving them his life savings." ✼ JD

"Walter did stay after the wedding and completed his younger brother's project. He then took the motor bike for its first spin, and with this he was hooked. He never went back to Kansas. Our two inventors were now three and they continued building motorcycles in my grandparents' basement. This went on until my great-grandmother, Margaret, just could not stand the mess anymore. They had also managed to take over their father's basement woodshop, where he would craft custom furniture. Sharing the basement put this quiet, dour Scotsman at his wit's end. This all led to them getting evicted!" ✼ JD

"William C. Davidson built a nice size shed in his backyard. It was 10 feet by 15 feet with a couple of windows and a small stove for heat. Now, I think he built it for his own carpentry projects, but maybe he built it for his kids, sensing they were going to need a workshop outside the house. Well, nonetheless, after the boys got the boot from the basement, the shed became the first Harley-Davidson factory! Their older sister, Janet, even painted their company name on the door." ▨ JDO

(From left to right) **James McLay, Janet Davidson, Margaret Davidson, Elizabeth Davidson, and William C. Davidson.**

"I often wondered if Janet painted the letters on the little factory door to make her brothers feel like they were doing something important. Do you think she really thought they were actually going to make motorcycles that would be loved all over the world? Janet was creative in her own way too, and many say she created the first H-D logo in 1910. Janet never married and took care of whomever in the family got sick. In 1930, she gave $50,000 to the Boy's and Girl's Club of Milwaukee." ❋ JD

"Arthur Davidson and Bill Harley had full-time jobs, and so this left Walter by himself during the day to work on their idea of the perfect motorcycle. He turned all his energy and drive into accomplishing this goal. They would work together at night, and the oldest Davidson, William, who worked full-time at the railroad in the tool room, pitched in when he could." ❋ JD

ABOVE: Young man looking at one of the first Harley-Davidson motorcycles in front of the famous shed.

RIGHT: The first Harley-Davidson factory.

"They grew the company quickly, and built this small factory on nearby Chestnut Street. Older brother William Davidson quit his job as foreman of the tool room at the Milwaukee Road and joined the busy little company." JDO

"They had one problem after the building was completed. A railroad fellow stopped by and informed them that their building was too close to the tracks and would have to be torn down. What did they do? They got everyone together, picked it up and moved it a couple feet over! No lawyers needed, job done." JD

The first real factory was built in late 1906.

An early company photo in front of the new factory in 1907. Walter Davidson (far right), William Davidson (second from right, standing), Arthur Davidson (third from right, kneeling). William Harley was at college studying for an engineering degree.

"The early workers at Harley-Davidson were like family. Many of them had worked in the railroad shops with the Davidson boys and their father William, who was a carpenter there. If a worker wanted a home built and could get the lumber, the senior William Davidson, my great-great-grandfather, would build it for him." JDO

"If an employee would recommend a member of their family for a job opening, he or she had a good chance of being hired. It then kind of became their responsibility to make sure their relative learned the ropes and worked hard. This accounted for two and three generations of some families working at Harley-Davidson. Harley-Davidson would hire people who were known by the other employees before they would hire a stranger." JD

ABOVE: Walter Davidson (second from the left in the front row) at the Catskill Mountain Endurance and Reliability Run in New York, 1908.

OPPOSITE: Walter Davidson just before leaving to ride to the factory.

"In 1908 my grandfather, Walter, entered the Catskill Mountain Endurance and Reliability Run. It was in New York, far from Milwaukee and his small motorcycle company. It was a lengthy 365-mile contest that required a rider to navigate a predetermined course on a specific schedule. Not only did my grandfather complete the course, but as legend goes, he also stopped and helped other riders along the way!" ✹ JD

"My great-grandfather, Walter, won the contest with a better than perfect score of 1,000 plus 5! A fact that makes this even more amazing is that he refused a chase vehicle or any kind of support during the event. His victory in that grueling endurance run helped establish Harley-Davidson on the East Coast. This was big Indian motorcycle territory at that time, and H-D was only considered a cowboy machine from out west." ▧ JDO

CHAPTER 2

BUILDING the FAMILY BUSINESS

"Growth was steady. In the first decade, after the days when motorcycles were built in the shed, the company doubled the number of square feet of factory floor space every year!" ⬥ JDO

"The employees were all proud, dedicated workers. The founders worked right by their sides and everyone was considered an equal. They all worked together and played together—although there wasn't much time for play. They worked ten hours a day during the week and eight on Saturday." ✷ JD

OPPOSITE: (Left to right) William S. Harley, Frank Ollerman and Walter Davidson) out for a ride in 1914.

RIGHT: Arthur
Davidson, Walter
Davidson, William S.
Harley and William
Davidson (left to right).

**THE HARLEY-DAVIDSON
MOTOR CYCLE**

MANUFACTURED BY

HARLEY-DAVIDSON MOTOR CO.
MILWAUKEE, WISCONSIN

ABOVE: The winged
hourglass was used
in the early days,
pre-1910, as a logo. It
symbolized Harley-
Davidson's ability to
conquer space and time.

"They all started out as tradesman. Arthur was a pattern maker. Walter was a machinist, electrician and a mechanic. William S. Harley was a draftsman. William Davidson, who had the nickname of Scotty, was a tool and die maker." ✱ JD

"The only founder to have a college degree was William S. Harley. He went to the University of Wisconsin at Madison and studied combustion engines. He was a very smart man and realized that the company would only be successful if its machines had superior design and engineering." ✱ JDO

"The factory had one door clearly marked 'shop' and another clearly marked 'office,' but nobody seemed to care. Everybody just used the shop door because no one was treated better than anyone else. They all worked as equals. This even included the founders." ✱ JD

Arthur Davidson (right)
delivers an early mail
delivery cycle in 1906. The
postal carrier was Pete
Olson of Cambridge, WI.

OPPOSITE: Arthur Davidson, the company's sales manager, explains selling points to the company salesmen in 1913.

LEFT: Arthur sits with the growing sales force on the steps of the ever-expanding Harley-Davidson factory in 1913.

Out in Eugene, Oregon, our dealers e Fisk & Tibbetts. Their original con-

trebled his contract.

The Weaver-Ebling Automobile Com-

Sales Manager Wears Broad Smile All The Time, These Happy Days

Sales Manager Davidson wears a broad smile these days; and it is not entirely due to the trainloads of Harley-Davidsons going out from the factory, either.

The fact is—maybe you have heard it already through the trade papers—Arthur Davidson has a little boy. The date of the event was March 28th.

Talk about your proud fathers! You remember that, less than a year ago "Bill" Harley passed the cigars upon the arrival of a little girl—his first is a boy—and that at about the same time Walter Davidson showed up one day and announced the arrival of his second son.

"Bill" Davidson listened with amused toleration to the hot argument as to whether it was better to have two boys, or a boy and a girl, because he has five—as many as they did, combined. Now they have him beat by one.

The Harley-Davidson family certainly is growing. Last summer *Motorcycling* said the stork ought to be adopted as the family crest. Good idea—we agree.

tract was for ten machines. We already have shipped them ten and they had two on order at the time this article was writ-

pany 2230 Broadway, New York City, demanded an increase of seventy machines on its 1914 contract. Apparently the

"Bill Knuth is a legend in Harley-Davidson company history. He was recruited by Arthur Davidson to sell new H-D motorcycles in his existing repair shop in 1925." JDO

Bill Knuth (far right) in his shop, Knuth Cycle Co., on Fond du Lac Avenue, Milwaukee, WI.

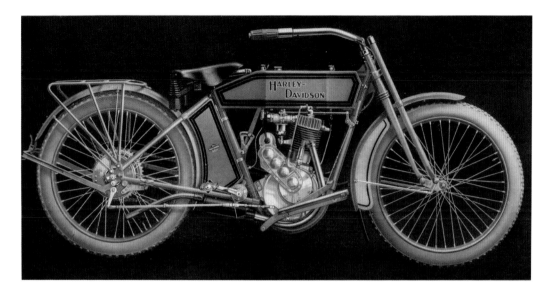

ABOVE LEFT: 1914 Harley-Davidson Model 10B with five horsepower and chain drive. Price was $210.

ABOVE RIGHT: Walter Davidson going over plans for the 1912 addition in his usual meticulous manner.

LEFT: Work being done on another factory addition in 1912.

"My great-grandfather, Walter Davidson, enjoyed riding on two wheels his whole life. When he was young, before combustion engines, he was an avid bicyclist. He even won several local races in Milwaukee." JDO

"Walter was known to take new motorcycles out and test them for speed by racing the trains that ran on the tracks behind the factory. Sometimes he would keep going all the way to Madison!" JD

"William Harley was the factory's chief engineer. He was responsible for countless design innovations in motorcycling, and was awarded many patents for his ideas. He and Walter would spend many long afternoons riding new motorcycles together and then critiquing their performance." JDO

"My grandfather, Walter, was a perfectionist in everything he did and this is why they made him the president of their company. He demanded quality. When he was at home, he was relaxed and fun, but at work it was all business." JD

ABOVE: Walter and William sit and discuss how the new models performed in 1913.

OPPOSITE: Walter Davidson and William Harley out for a ride in 1913.

Walter Davidson inspects the new two-story press that had just been installed. Large equipment like this was the reason more space was continually needed.

NEW ZEALAND

LEFT: Arthur and Clara with son, Arthur Harley Davidson, who was born in 1914.

FAR LEFT: Arthur and his wife, Clara, in New Zealand setting up a new dealership.

"Beginning in 1904, Arthur Davidson spent most of his time setting up new dealerships all over the world. He became close friends with his dealers and would tell his brothers and William Harley that if the dealers make money, so will Harley-Davidson. He considered his dealers the gold of the future and would go to their dealerships himself whenever there was a problem." ▦ JDO

"Arthur admired his best friend, William S. Harley, so much that he named his first son after him, Arthur Harley Davidson! Interesting side note is that young Arthur went to college and studied languages so he could join his father's company and travel the world setting up dealerships. He was the youngest of the founders' children, so by the time he graduated, the other children were already working at the company. Young Arthur went to the factory and expected his father to welcome him into the family business. It was not to be. His father said, ' No, there are already too many cooks in the kitchen!' Young Arthur was devastated, but he then went and started his own company called Wenthe-Davidson. Young Arthur's company is still going strong today." ✳ JD

RIGHT: Here is the entire line of Harley-Davidsons in 1914. At the end of the line is the unique package truck.

OPPOSITE: Gertrude H. Hoffman in the sidecar with Carl Lang on the far right in front of Lang's Harley-Davidson dealership in Chicago in 1922.

"Carl Herman Lang was Harley-Davidson's first dealer. He opened his shop in Chicago in 1905 after a stint as a piano tool manufacturer. The story goes that he heard about Harley and the Davidson brothers building motorcycles up in Milwaukee and solicited them to sell their new motorcycles. This turned out to be a good thing for all. In the early years, most all machines the Motor Company sold went through Lang's dealership. Lang was an instrumental force behind the early growth years of Harley-Davidson and even became a shareholder. His input was greatly respected, and therefore he was placed on the company's board of directors for many years." ▨ JDO

"Gertrude Hoffman was a popular vaudeville dancer and a successful choreographer. She danced with a suggestive and risqué style that stirred up a lot of attention in theatres across the country. Numerous times she was actually arrested when local authorities became offended by her routines. She actually became famous imitating Anna Held in a Florenz Ziegfeld production." ✿ JD

An early Harley-Davidson dealership.

CHAPTER 3
STORIED CAREERS

"My grandfather Walter was extremely ethical. If he said he would do something, you didn't need to get it in writing. His word was as good as gold. He sat on the boards at many of Wisconsin's largest companies. He was well respected for his business skills and knowledge. I was told a story about a particular board meeting at a local bank. The bank's president got up and bawled out an employee in front of the entire group. Walter did not like this at all and stood up and bawled out the president himself! He told him that kind of thing was to be done in private and then he resigned from the board." ✺ JD

**Walter Davidson
was always
ready for a ride.**

Proud father, Walter Davidson, holding his baby son, Gordon McLay, in 1911.

"My great-grandfather, Walter, cared not only about his own thriving company, but also about the success of other young enterprises. When the Depression came, many companies began struggling to survive. If Harley-Davidson had any smaller projects that could be farmed out, Walter would hand them off to other local companies to help them survive too. When times got better, this made for some loyal friends and a strong industrial community." 🔲 JDO

"William S. Harley was a quiet gentleman who turned gray at a young age. For a period of time the motorcycles he designed and Harley-Davidson manufactured were known on the street as Silent Gray Fellows. Most people thought it was because they were gray in color and very quiet. However, many at the factory thought the nickname was a tribute to William S. Harley because he was usually silent and had gray hair at a very young age." ❈ JD

"Sarah Harley used to like to brag that during his career in the motorcycle business her grandfather, William S. Harley, was granted 67 patents for his innovative design ideas!" ❈ JD

ABOVE: William S. Harley (fifth from left in back row) with the service school of 1927.

RIGHT: A 1914 Harley-Davidson "Silent Gray Fellow."

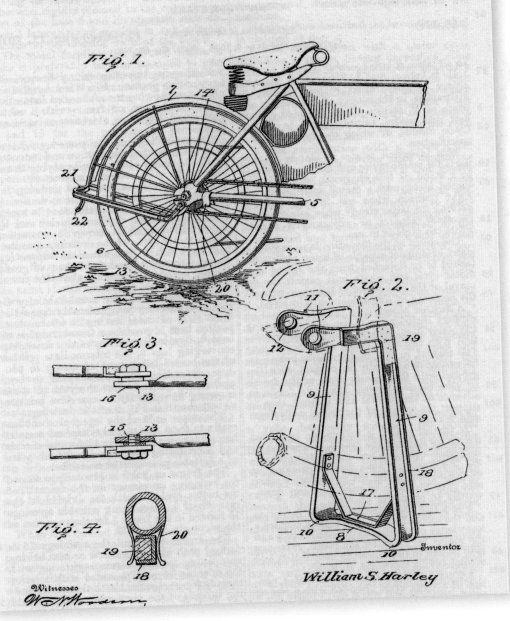

W. S. HARLEY.
MOTOR CYCLE STAND.
APPLICATION FILED JUNE 2, 1909.

946,037.

Patented Jan. 11, 1910.

Fig. 1.

Fig. 2.

Fig. 3.

Fig. 4.

Witnesses

Inventor

William S Harley

"William Harley loved to fish, hunt and draw in his spare time. He would often take my grandfather, Walter, out fishing with him because Walter had so much energy that he couldn't sit still to fish. This made him the perfect candidate to man the oars! People would see them out on the lake and would always notice William fishing and Walter rowing away." ❀ JD

ABOVE: Sketches by William S. Harley.

LEFT: One of the many patents that was awarded to William S. Harley.

"In the 1920s two young fellows from two separate shifts decided to make their own motorcycle by stealing each part one at a time. The employee on the first shift would hide a part. The second shift guy would then walk the part to the fence and hoist it over to his partner in crime from the first shift. This went on for a long time. Finally they had all the pieces except for the most important one, the engine. They didn't take just any engine, but a special racing one, of which only a few were made. It came right out of William S. Harley's department, and William took great pride in his racing motors and quickly noticed this one missing. So when the second-shifter made his way to the fence to hoist the prize over to his partner, he was being followed by none other than Bill Davidson. Bill quietly approached the employee as he was lifting it over the fence and tapped him on the shoulder. 'May I help you?' is all he asked. This was the end of two careers at Harley-Davidson." ✸ JD

ABOVE: Bill Davidson with William S. Harley in the background.

William Harley and Arthur Davidson after a round of golf.

"William S. Harley also loved to play golf. Many days he worked until dusk so by the time he would get to the golf course it would be getting dark. He enlisted his best friend's son, Arthur Harley Davidson, to come along and wear a white T-shirt. He would send him out on the course to stand near the green so Bill would know where to aim. Many a time young Arthur had to duck to keep from being hit by a well-struck golf ball. But after the game Bill would always buy young Arthur a soda pop. How could young Arthur refuse anyway, since Harley was his middle name!" JDO

A member of Arthur Davidson's loyal sales force.

"As legend goes, William Davidson, who was in charge of manufacturing, would give a holiday turkey to every worker. When the Depression came in the 1930s, much to his dismay he had to lay many people off. Even though they were not at work when Thanksgiving came around, they still received a turkey from Bill. William Davidson was better known by his employees and most everyone as 'Old Bill,' a big man with a big heart." ⬚ JDO

William Harley (left), William Davidson (in sidecar) and Stanley Malanowski who was the H-D dealer from Laconia, NH. The two Bills were on a trip out East in 1923.

William Harley points something out to William Davidson in the sidecar while traveling on the East Coast in 1923.

"Bill Davidson was always on the shop floor and knew all the employees and their families by their names. When an employee fell on hard times financially, Bill Davidson would lend him enough money to get by. He would keep track of the loans in a little black book that he always carried in his jacket pocket. He never asked for the money back. Even though years would go by, the employee always remembered what Bill had done for him. He would show up one day with the money and tell him thanks for the trust. Bill died in 1937. Many people have said that his heart was broken when the shop unionized. He always felt he had taken great care of the workers and never understood why some of them thought they needed a union to represent them." ❋ JD

"When the workers at Harley-Davidson did an especially good job, my grandfather, Walter, would go up on the roof and raise a flag. It would be seen down the street at the Gettelman Brewery and Fredrick 'Fritzy' Gettelman would hitch up the horse to the wagon and load up a fresh, ice-cold, barrel of beer. He would then personally deliver it to the Harley-Davidson factory and everyone would celebrate. My grandfather was good friends with Fritzy Gettelman. I think they were as similar as they were different. They both ran major companies and were both known to be very ethical and men of their word. They were both inventors by nature. Fritzy designed the first snowplow as well as numerous other inventions, including the first steel beer barrel. He promised another local company, A. O. Smith, the rights to manufacturer these steel barrels and stood by his word even after he was offered one million dollars by an out-of-town company for the rights. Now that's a man of his word!" ✳ JD

"I love the stories about Fritzy Gettelman. He was a larger-than-life guy. Even at the young age of 22, he was his father's chief assistant and in charge of all brewery operations. When prohibition ended, he aggressively went out and signed up taverns to carry their family brew. He signed up some 35 on his own and would stop personally at each one quite often to check on things and, of course, have a mug of beer. He loved cigars and some say he would smoke an entire box in a day! He would canvas Milwaukee with his dog Rex, a spaniel, in his car of choice, a Packard. He went on to be president of the Gettelman Brewery after his father and brother took a turn." ▨ JDO

**OPPOSITE: Walter
Davidson and Fredrick
Gettelman enjoying
a cold brew. Fredrick
has his trademark
cigar burning.**

**An advertisement
from 1920.**

"My family loved the Gettelman's product and they loved ours as well. There were three Gettelmans in the Milwaukee Motorcycle Club, which was a H-D-only club. When prohibition ended, one of the first half-barrels produced was set aside for the club. It was then picked up in Bill Knuth's sidecar rig and delivered to their clubhouse! Man, I would have liked to have been at that party!" ▨ JDO

Invitation for a party hosted by Walter and Emma Davidson.

"All the founders worked hard and played hard. My grandfather, Walter, and grandmother, Emma, loved having parties for their many friends. These parties were well planned with creative themes. All the details were important, from the food to invitations. Maybe this is how my grandfather relaxed after spending so much time at the factory. My grandmother used to say she was lucky if her husband would be home by 8 p.m. during a work week. In the beginning years they also worked on Saturdays and considered it just another work day." ✽ JD

"I always love to hear the stories about the parties that my grandparents and great-grandparents used to host. They sound like such productions and must have really been fun to attend. The guest lists always included the movers and shakers of Milwaukee." ▨ JDO

(Left to right) William Davidson, Walter Davidson, Arthur Davidson and William S. Harley.

"I think the company really thrived because each of the founders had his own set of skills and developed them to the fullest. They each excelled by using their own particular gift." ❀ JD

"Arthur loved to travel and had a wonderful gift of gab. This made him perfect to run the sales side of things. Bill Davidson liked to be on the shop floor, which fit perfectly with his tool-making background. My great-grandfather was a perfectionist and a sharp businessman. He was an avid reader and constantly tried to learn all he could. William S. Harley just wanted to be left alone so he could get his brilliant ideas out of his head and onto paper." ▢ JDO

"For sport, the founders loved hunting and fishing, but they also had hobbies that were more relaxing. Arthur Davidson loved farming, William Harley enjoyed drawing wildlife, William Davidson was known for his beautiful gardens, and my great-grandfather, Walter, was a voracious reader." ▢ JDO

Stella Forge (right) with friend, Liz Moyle, in February 1934, Nagawicka Lake.

"Stella Forge was the switchboard operator at H-D forever! She lived close to the factory and walked to work every day. When she wasn't at work, she was at our house and everyone thought of her as one of the family. Everyone always knew that if you wanted to know where any of the Davidsons or Harleys were, all you had to do was ask Stella. She also controlled who got in to see them at work, so the salesmen learned real quick that it was a smart idea to make friends with Stella." ❋ JD

"Crystal Haydel was my grandfather Walter Davidson's secretary and unofficial office manager. She started her long career with the company in 1908 and became very loyal to my grandfather. He trusted her with many of his daily chores, including signing his name when he was too busy or out of the office. He had her practice his signature until it was a spot-on match." ❋ JD

"Crystal had her hands in everything at the Motor Company. She kept all the books, handled payroll and even helped hire and sometimes fire workers. She was a one-woman accounting and human resources department! She was even on the board of directors. From what I understand, she was the first woman to register a motorcycle for road use in the state of Wisconsin!" ▨ JDO

Crystal Haydel skiing in 1940.

"I simply love the fact that my grandfather and his brothers were best friends their whole lives. They not only worked together, but also spent their fun time hunting, fishing and playing golf together. William Harley wasn't only a business partner, but family as well. They truly thought of him as their brother. They liked him so much they put his name first on the tank!" ❀ JD

The four founders (left to right), William Davidson, Walter Davidson, Arthur Davidson and William Harley.

CHAPTER 4

FOLLOWING FATHER

Gordon McLay
Davidson, Walter
Davidson's eldest son.

(Left to right) Young
Walter C., Robert
and Gordon, sons
of founder Walter
Davidson.

"The sons of the founders started being seen around the company when they were youngsters. They would be put to work emptying waste baskets, sweeping floors and running errands for their fathers. There was a saying in our family, 'If you want to see your father, run down to the factory!'" ✺ JD

(Left to right) Walter C., Gordon and Allan Davidson on the road in 1929.

"In 1929, the sons of the founders somehow talked their fathers into letting them take a road trip to the West Coast. Gordon was the oldest at 17. They were called the three musketeers. They returned with many stories of adventure, most of which could only be told at the factory, far from the ears of their mothers!" ✻ JD

"Of course their dads had them take the latest-model bikes and required them to visit all the dealers along the way. Our young adventures never realized that they were not only on a fun vacation, but they were also advertising for the family business! All the founders' children went to college, but that only went so far with their fathers. The general theory at the Motor Company was education is nice, but there is no substitute for shop experience. All were required to start at the bottom wearing a pair of overalls and getting their hands greasy." ▨ JDO

Children of the founders getting ready for a chilly ride in Milwaukee. (Left to right) Walter C. and Gordon (sons of Walter Davidson), William (son of William Davidson) and William J. (son of William S. Harley) in 1928.

Gordon Davidson in his parent's basement in 1934.

"My father, Gordon, was constantly compared to his uncle, Bill Davidson. They both liked to spend most of their time on the shop floor. They both felt that all the people who worked at their company every day were what made it successful. They both liked to know each employee's name, and when they saw them in the morning would thank them for coming to work." ❀ JD

"I think that my grandfather's ability to relate to all the employees and the fact that he didn't like to stay in his office much made him perfect to be the head of manufacturing at the Motor Company." ▨ JDO

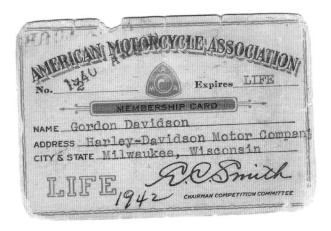

"I heard a great story about my grandfather, Gordon, from one of his longtime line workers. It seems this worker had been building his own motorcycle at home for years. He would report his progress to my grandfather weekly. One day he reported that his project was almost complete. All he had to do now was to save enough money for the seat. Gordon then asked him to point out what style seat he really wanted. He did. Gordon then grabbed the seat off the line and took out his pocket knife. He proceeded to put a scratch down the back side of the seat. He told his loyal employee that this was unfortunate because the seat could no longer be used. He then told him to take it home and maybe he could find a use for it." ▨ JDO

Gordon Davidson's pocket knife that he always carried.

Harley-Davidson company picnic in 1937. Could that be Gordon Davidson with the rolled-up pants and sporting the saddle shoes?

"It is said that everyone at H-D worked hard, but they also liked to play hard. They worked together and often partied together as well!" 🔲 JDO

"If you worked at H-D you usually had a job for life, unless you were a woman and wanted to get married. There was an unwritten rule that no married women were allowed to work at the factory. This continued even into the 1950s. The only reason for this that I have ever heard was because the founders were from the old school and believed a woman who was married belonged at home cooking and taking care of the children. Today that would not go over so well." ❈ JD

Gordon Davidson attends a sales convention in 1930.

Harley-Davidson's company picnic in 1941. Gordon Davidson's wife, Doris, is sitting on the left in the foreground.

"My father married his childhood sweetheart after they finished college. He attended the Wharton School of Business at the University of Pennsylvania and majored in finance. My mother went to University of Wisconsin at Madison and majored in physical education." ❀ JD

"My father, Gordon, was headed home from the factory one cold winter day. It was one of the coldest days of that year so he actually took his car to work instead of a motorcycle. When he stopped at the corner, he saw one of his employees waiting for the bus. He noticed that the fellow wasn't wearing a jacket, so he rolled down his window and asked him why. The longtime employee explained things were a little tight at home so he gave his winter jacket to his son. My dad didn't think twice. He pulled off his jacket and tossed it out the window and told him, 'Merry Christmas!' The man quickly slipped on the jacket and later noticed there were two twenty-dollar bills in the pocket. Being an honest sort of guy, he went and found Gordon and thanked him for the jacket. He then tried to return the money, but my father wouldn't take it and once again said, 'Merry Christmas!'" ❀ JD

Gordon Davidson on the factory floor in 1956 with Ed Meyer standing to the left of tool-and-die apprentice Chuck Moravec (wearing apron).

Ray Wolf on his last day of work at Harley-Davidson in 2008.

Jerry Zielinski working as a layout inspector in the metrology lab at Harley-Davidson in 1990.

"Ray Wolf, a Motor Company retiree, told me a great story. One day his department was shut down to have the ceiling painted. My father Gordon and William H. Davidson were walking out of the factory to go to lunch. This is when Ray and his coworker had a smart idea to play a prank. Everyone worked hard, but pulling a fast one on each other did happen from time to time. Well, it seems Ray and his fellow coconspirator took rolls of toilet paper and held them between their fingers. They then let the dangling ends of the rolls get caught up in an exhaust fan. The fan pulled all the paper off the rolls and proceeded to turn it into confetti that fell down to the sidewalk below. Gordon and Bill were showered in toilet paper confetti. Ray said that my grandfather laughed and came back from lunch smiling." ▨ JDO

"Jerry Zielinski, another employee, told me a funny story that happened during third shift at the Capital Drive plant. During a lunch break a rumor spread that one of the guys was going to streak through the factory. So after lunch the guys lined the main aisle and waited for a minute or two. Then, sure enough, a guy driving an electric cart and wearing nothing but a ski mask and his work boots came buzzing through the factory! The streaker was hooting and all the guys were laughing and then the cart ran out of juice and stopped! The naked guy had to jump off his chariot and quickly disappeared into the crowd. The foreman was not happy about all the commotion and wanted to know who the exhibitionist was. Everybody knew, but to this day, the streaker's identity has remained a secret. ✳ JD

LEFT: Gordon Davidson breaking ground for the new Capital Drive addition in the early 1950s. Sitting on the motorcycle is David Morton.

OPPOSITE: Gordon Davidson dancing with his wife, Doris.

"My father loved the plant on Capital Drive, as it was acquired on his watch and he was very proud of it. One day in 1947 my dad took the whole family on a train ride to a secret destination. The train was full of dealers who were in town for a convention. We left from the Juneau Avenue plant and set out across town. I thought maybe we were going to a horse ranch in the mountains! As it turned out the secret destination was the newly opened Capital Drive plant. The dealers all loved it, but I was secretly bummed out." ✳ JD

"My dad loved to dance. One of his favorite special moves that he made up was what he called the 'sneak' dance. He would bend down low with my mother and sneak across the dance floor. I would love it when he would ask me to be his partner. Everyone else on the dance floor would chuckle when they saw us coming. It was especially a big hit at my wedding." ✳ JD

"In the family tradition, all the founders children also loved to have parties. In fact, our basement had a wine/liquor room with a large bar, a room with gambling tables and even a room with real slot machines! I remember on the walls were calendar girls with very little on. No wonder my friends would like to go down there and play. My parents had lots of parties at our house, but the kids were always sent off to bed. I would sneak halfway down the stairs and listen to all the fun. When my dad turned 50 years old, his friends threw a big party. I was old enough to go to that party and I remember many people telling stories and singing songs. It was really neat. No one knew that in a short six years this vibrant young man would be gone." ✸ JD

Invitation for Gordon McLay Davidson's 50th birthday party in 1961.

Two score and ten years ago there was brought forth upon this continent a new baby, conceived and dedicated to the proposition of being a mixed-up little kid.

Now (half a century later) he is engaged in planning a great celebration of that birth, testing whether that kid, or any other kids, can keep on mixing it up and long endure. It is altogether fitting and proper that he should do this.

But in a larger sense, he cannot dedicate, he cannot consecrate, he cannot celebrate this event alone. His brave friends who have struggled here can celebrate it far above his poor power to add or detract. The world will little note or long remember what is said here, but he hopes his friends will not forget what they did here on his 50th celebration. This kid is dedicated to the great task before him and he highly resolves that this birthday party shall not be in vain. He is resolved that this 50th celebration of the people, by the people, and for the people shall be full of mixed-up fun, mixed-up drinks, given by that mixed-up kid, Gordon, on the battlefield of Pewaukee Lake at Yacht Club Lanes on July 28, 1961.

Cocktails at 7. Food later. RSVP, 6561 Washington Circle, Wauwatosa, Wis.

GORDON & DORIS DAVIDSON

Gordon M. Davidson.

"The employees liked and respected my dad, just like they had his uncle, Bill Davidson. When my father lost his battle with cancer in 1967, the most touching thing for me was the number of people who filled the funeral parlor. Not only did the company managers show, but all the shift guys as well. I remember crying and I remember all those shop guys crying right with me." ❋ JD

"I wish my grandfather would have lived longer. I love hearing stories about him from my mom and dad. I remember times at Pewaukee Lake, and we were always having fun." ▨ JDO

"Walter C. was my grandparents' middle child and he liked to be mischievous. He was a real handful. His older brother, Gordon, my father, did everything he was told to do. Walter, on the other hand, marched to the beat of his own drum." ✸ JD

"Walter C. would go on to have a long career with H-D. Founder Arthur Davidson took young Walter C. under his wing and taught him everything about motorcycle sales. This gave him an outlet for all his energy and took him to all corners of the world! He liked people just like his uncle Arthur did, and enjoyed entertaining." ▨ JDO

Young Walter C. Davidson with his dog.

"My grandfather, Gordon's brother, Walter C., loved sports cars. He would get a new one every so often. One day he came to work in a beautiful new Corvette. A rather new H-D employee was walking in the front door of the factory for work when he saw Walter pull up. He stopped in his tracks and yelled to Walter, 'Wow, that's some beaut!' Walter smiled, tossed him the car keys and said, 'Why don't you take it for a spin?' The young brake operator couldn't believe his ears, but jumped in, squealed the tires and sped off. He drove around the block a few times, waving and beeping the horn at everyone." ▨ JDO

ABOVE: One of Walter C.'s favorite Corvettes.

RIGHT: Walter C. Davidson stands proud in 1934.

"My friend Bob Jameson, son of the legendary H-D employee Hap Jameson, told me a great story. Bob said it all started when my father, Gordon, and his brother, Walter, were up in Shawano, WI, for a big motorcycle rally. They stopped at a local watering hole for a quick beer, but ended up staying awhile. While they were in the tavern, some guys in the group decided to play a joke on Walter. They removed the sidecar that was attached to Walter's motorcycle and moved the cycle over so that it would be leaning against a small tree in the parking lot. Then they proceeded to reattach the sidecar so the small tree was between the bike and the sidecar. When Walter came out to ride back to the rally and saw the tree growing out of his motorcycle, he laughed and laughed. He said, 'I didn't think I was in there that long.'" ❋ JD

While visiting a dealership in Japan, Walter C. Davidson sits on one of the motorcycles manufactured during his father's days with the Motor Co.

Walter C. Davidson dressed in drag at a charity event.

"Harley-Davidson had grown into a world-renowned company and the sons of the founders were well respected in society. They were asked, and often agreed, to lead fundraisers for many different causes in the Milwaukee area. Work was important, but charitable causes were too." ▨ JDO

"Between 1959 and 1965 a bunch of employees had factory bikes and formed the Road and Tracker Club. These employees were from all different departments and would rather ride than eat lunch. They would take off for the lunch hour and ride on and off road. The only rule was it had to be above ten degrees. There weren't any rules on where they could ride, so they would find the roughest areas. The guys would come back full of mud and grease, but with big smiles on their faces. Walter C. would look at the bikes and say, 'How could you guys have made such a mess in such a short time?'" ✽ JD

William S. Harley in
the middle with his son
John on his right.

(Left to right) Chief
Engineer William
Harley, Inspector
Fenker of the U.S.
Army Quartermaster
Corps and President
Walter Davidson
looking over a few
of the 110 new 1932
models purchased for
the army.

"Sarah Harley told me a great story about her dad and her grandfather. At the beginning of World War II, William S. Harley was visiting Fort Knox where his son John was stationed. There was a discussion between the generals on what vehicle would do better in the war on the rugged ground, a Jeep or a Harley-Davidson. They decided to put them to the test. They found the muddiest, roughest ground and made a course. Each tried to run through it. The Jeep got stuck every time and the Harley-Davidson went through without any trouble. From then on they used that course for training the army's motorcycle division. John Harley became the head of motorcycle training. He was also in charge of training the mechanics in the army on how to fix and work on the motorcycles." ❋ JD

LEFT: William James Harley, the oldest son of founder William S. Harley.

William James Harley

"William James Harley followed in his father's footsteps and earned a mechanical engineering degree from the University of Wisconsin at Madison. He then joined H-D and eventually would take over as chief engineer after his father died. He had many motorcycling adventures, mostly with his lifetime friend William H. Davidson. From riding solo in grueling endurance races to traveling across the country with William H. in a sidecar, the two tried it all." ❁ JD

"One of the stories that I have heard about William James Harley is about his unselfish behavior. One time he and his pal William H. Davidson were riding in the Jack Pine Enduro, which is a two-day cross-country event in Michigan, when Davidson looked over at his friend and said, 'I think I have a chance at winning, but my stopwatch broke.' Harley, without saying a word, removed his own and gave it to his best friend, who then went on to win. This was typical of William James Harley." ▨ JDO

"William H. Davidson was the oldest son of founder William Davidson. Going with family traditions, he also loved to ride. He and founder William Harley's oldest son were best friends. They went on many motorcycle adventures together. They also both liked to compete in endurance runs and other racing events." ✺ JD

"William H. Davidson, who is Willie G. Davidson's father, would go on to have a lengthy H-D career. He patterned himself after my grandfather, Walter Davidson, in many ways and the two became quite close. In 1942 one of my grandfather's last orders was to name William H. Davidson to take his place as president of the Motor Company." ✺ JD

William H. Davidson wins the Jack Pine Enduro in 1930.

CHAPTER 5

SCOTLAND

"The Davidson family had a humble beginning. Alexander Davidson was a wheelwright who married Margaret Scott. They lived in Scotland with their six children until 1858. This was the year they decided life would be better in America and this would give their children a brighter future. One of their sons, Alexander Jr., was a very gifted student, and they thought America would be the place for him to succeed. Unfortunately, young Alexander contracted ship's fever on the long journey across the ocean and died shortly after arriving in the United States." ❋ JD

"The promise of opportunity did hold true for the rest of the Davidsons. Alexander got a good job with the railroad and this is what brought them to Milwaukee, WI. One of their children, William C., also had a productive career with the railroad. But there is no doubt that William's sons left the biggest footprint on the world when they started the Harley-Davidson Motor Company that is still flourishing today." ❖ JDO

Margaret and Alexander Davidson.

(LEFT TO RIGHT FROM OPPOSITE PAGE)

Walter Davidson's sons, Walter C. and Gordon McLay, 1916.

Arthur Harley Davidson, Arthur Davidson's son, 1918.

Barbara Davidson and sister, Jean, get their turn in the Scottish suits.

"My family has always been very proud of its Scottish heritage. My grandfather had two traditional outfits sent over from Scotland. He would have his children dress up in them for parades and special events. It gave him great enjoyment to show his Scottish pride." JD

"The kids don't look too thrilled in having to be dressed up Scottish style, but I am sure my great-grandfather really enjoyed it." JDO

BELOW: William McLay Oeflein and sister, Susan.

"The tradition continues. When children in our family get big enough, they are asked to wear the Scottish outfits that were originally brought to America by my grandfather, Walter Davidson. I hope the tradition continues forever." ✻ JD

ABOVE: Peter John Oeflein.

LEFT: Jon Davidson Oeflein with his sister, Lori Jean.

ABOVE: Max McLay Oeflein with sister, Annie.

RIGHT: Nicolas Davidson Oeflein.

BELOW: Jean Davidson and Bruce Davidson at Scottish Fest.

"My cousin Bruce and I love our Scottish heritage. Every year we are attend the Scottish Fest in Wisconsin. It is a lot of fun with traditional activities and contests. We are honored to carry the flame for the Davidson clan." ✽ JD

"In early 2008, Mike Sinclair, a lifelong Harley-Davidson enthusiast, discovered that a certain cottage in a beautiful area of Scotland was under threat of being torn down. Research showed that this cottage was the home of Alexander [Sandy] Davidson and his wife Margaret. One of their children was William C., who became the father of the three Davidson boys who started Harley-Davidson. Mike wanted to save the cottage, so he recruited his friends Maggie Sherrit and Keith Macintosh, who quickly shared his dream. They came to Milwaukee and met with me. I loved their plans to restore my great-great-grandparents' home.

They had read my books so they knew some of the history. They wanted to know more, so I took them to spend the afternoon with Arthur Harley Davidson, who is the son of founder Arthur Davidson. They listened to him tell all the wonderful stories that I always enjoyed hearing. They returned to Scotland and proceeded to restore the cottage. Now motorcycle enthusiasts can visit and see how the pioneering Davidsons would have lived in the 1850s. It was nice to hear Maggie say that 'It was in Milwaukee that we were lucky to meet one of our main sources of inspiration, Jean Davidson.'" ✻ JD

Alexander Davidson's family cottage located close to the sleepy village of Aberlemno, Scotland, as it was in 2008.

(Left to right) Keith Macintosh, Maggie Sherrit and Mike Sinclair in front of the refurbished cottage in 2012.

ABOVE: Arthur Davidson descendant, Heather McDonell, visiting her great-great-great-great-grandfather's cottage on her honeymoon in 2012.

RIGHT: (Left to right) Jean Davidson, Arthur Harley Davidson and Maggie Sherrit.

"I am glad to see that my relative's cottage has become a pilgrimage site for H-D enthusiasts from around the world. Just think that if Alexander and his family never made the long, arduous journey from Scotland to America, how different so many people's lives would be. There never would have been a Harley-Davidson Motor Company." ▨ JDO

CHAPTER 6

THE LAKES

LEFT: Fishing and motorcycling, a perfect combination for fun! Now and back in 1923.

OPPOSITE: (Left to right) William Davidson and William S. Harley, Harley-Davidson founders.

"Where do you go to relax? Well the founders remembered how much fun they had when they were boys going fishing. So, once they got their business up and running and they were confident it was a success, they returned to the water for a little rest in their spare time." ❀ JD

"My great-grandfather, Walter, built a beautiful home on Lake Michigan. William S. Harley chose Beaver Lake, William Davidson picked Pine Lake and for Arthur Davidson it was Lake Ripley." ▧ JDO

"The four founders remained good friends all their lives. This is a tough thing to do when in business together. They all worked together and lived close by in the city. Perhaps this is why they choose different lakes for their down time!" ❀ JD

**Walter Davidson with
sons Gordon and
Walter C. at Pewaukee
Lake, WI, in 1917.**

William Harley pulls while Arthur Davidson pushes.

"The founders were always trying to improve their product. This meant spending as much time in the saddle as possible. They would ride to work, ride in their spare time and ride to the lakes for fun. All the while paying attention to how their machines performed and making notes for back at the factory." ◈ JDO

"I always wondered why my grandfather and the other founders never changed out of their work cloths before going fishing. I bet they just didn't want to waste any of their precious spare time!" ✳ JD

DAVIDSONS, LAKE RIPLEY, WIS. 9904

ABOVE: Memorial sign in Cambridge, WI.

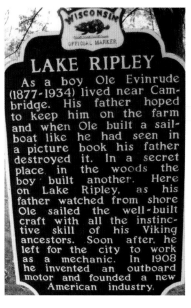

WISCONSIN OFFICIAL MARKER

LAKE RIPLEY

As a boy Ole Evinrude (1877-1934) lived near Cambridge. His father hoped to keep him on the farm and when Ole built a sailboat like he had seen in a picture book his father destroyed it. In a secret place in the woods the boy built another. Here on Lake Ripley, as his father watched from shore Ole sailed the well-built craft with all the instinctive skill of his Viking ancestors. Soon after, he left for the city to work as a mechanic. In 1908 he invented an outboard motor and founded a new American industry.

Arthur Davidson's lake home on Lake Ripley, WI.

"In true Scottish style, William C. Davidson, the father of the Davidson founders, married a Scottish girl named Margaret McFarlane. Margaret was from Cambridge, WI, where many Scottish families had settled because the hilly land resembled their Scottish homeland. After marrying William C., Margaret moved to Milwaukee to live with her new husband, but she never stopped going back to her home area, which included Lake Ripley." ❋ JD

"When Arthur Davidson was a young boy, he would spend summers with his grandparents in Cambridge. He would work on the neighbor's farm. In his spare time he would, of course, be on Lake Ripley and he grew to love this part of Wisconsin. This is where he met Ole Evinrude. It was the start of a lifelong friendship. Ole went on to build an outboard boat-motor empire, while Arthur concentrated on motorcycles. It is said that they had a pact not to compete with each other." ▦ JDO

"No one likes spending time at the lake more than kids do." ⬚ JDO

"Arthur H. would tell great stories about his days on Lake Ripley. He would say, 'Everyone always had lots of fun at the lake. Every day was filled with fun activities and making things. This was a time way before computers or video games. We made up our own fun. We went outside in the morning and didn't come back in the house until bedtime.'" ✿ JD

Arthur Harley Davidson (third from the left), his cousins John and William Marx, and his sister, Margaret (holding ball), at their Lake Ripley cottage in the 1920s.

**OPPOSITE: Walter
gives chase to his
eldest son, Gordon.**

**Mary Harley dreams of
driving an early outboard
motorboat on Beaver
Lake, WI.**

"My summers were spent on Pewaukee Lake. My dad rode his motorcycle 30 miles to the H-D plant every day, including Saturdays. Did I ever think about what it must have been like riding into the sun every morning and into the sun every night? No, I was busy having fun, swimming, sailing, waterskiing and even riding the neighbor's cows. I rode my first big motorcycle at 12, and I rode straight into Pewaukee Lake at full speed. It was the talk of the lake community. I didn't go back to Milwaukee until the day before school started. It seemed like another world at the lake." ❀ JD

ABOVE: Gordon Davidson with his wife, Doris, and daughter, Jean, at Pewaukee Lake, WI, in the summer of 1940.

TOP RIGHT: Doris Davidson sits on a pier in the sun.

BELOW RIGHT: Gordon Davidson with daughter, Jean, on the dock.

"My dad never wanted to be called 'dad' or 'father.' We called him Gordon. One time someone asked me if he was my stepfather. I said, 'No! He is my dad and my friend.' I think it was because he was so young-acting and always had fun at whatever he was doing. I still miss him every day." ✷ JD

RIGHT: Doris and Gordon Davidson with daughters, Jean and Barbara.

FAR RIGHT: Doris with youngest daughter, Christine, in the summer of 1950.

Jean Davidson having
fun on Pewaukee
Lake, Pewaukee,
WI, at age 16 with
summer boyfriend,
Bill Reckmeyer.

BELOW: John Oeflein in his favorite Chris Craft.

William gets ready for a ski run with John behind the wheel and Susan and Peter looking on.

"After I married John Oeflein and started a family of my own, we continued to enjoy summers on Pewaukee Lake at my parents' home. One weekend we went up to the North Woods with Willie G. Davidson and his wife, Nancy, for a long weekend. Our friend Bill Brunner, who worked at the factory, had decided to try his hand at the bar business. While everyone partied away at the new place, I ventured out to see the sights. I happened upon a beautiful lake property that I immediately fell in love with." ✳ JD

"My mom dragged my dad out of the bar and showed him this log home on Catfish Lake. Always a fan of fine craftsmanship and the woods, my dad was easily sold. This was the start of our own lake memories on Catfish Lake, in Eagle River, WI." ◻ JDO

Jon Davidson Oeflein in his boat in Eagle River, WI, in 1977. Along for the ride are Susan Winter (standing), Heidi Winter and John Meyer.

FAMILY WEDDINGS

CHAPTER 7

"Walter was the last founder to get married. He didn't want any distractions until he knew the company that he was president of was going to be successful." ✳ JD

WISCONSIN MOTORIST

Gave Him a Good Sendoff.

On Monday, Aug. 22, Walter Davidson, president of the Harley-Davidson Motor Co., Milwaukee, left the factory at about noon, time in his ordinary working clothes, supposedly to go to dinner. However, someone had put Mr. Davidson's friends at the factory wise to the fact that he was to be married at 1:30 o'clock. Inquiry proved this to be true, so a brigade was organized to go to the church and surprise Mr. Davidson.

About 12 motorcycles, most of them with exhaust whistles and a couple of automobiles also with siren horns, went to the church and got in just in time to make the performance interesting. What was intended to be a real quiet wedding, proved to be very much the opposite.

After the ceremony, the regiment that followed the cab to the bride's home, could be heard about four miles off. After keeping the newly-weds from catching the intended train, the friends of the young couple let them go to the depot and the bunch that went to the train was considerably larger than the original outfit. The send-off is something that will never be forgotten by any of the eye witnesses. There was said to be enough rice and old shoes in the Northwestern depot when the train pulled out to feed and shoe the city of Milwaukee, while the rear end of the Pullman bore a large sign upon which was written, "We Are Just Married."

At Chicago, the couple found that the telephone had beaten them and there was a large assemblage of Mr. Davidson's friends waiting for them there. Here Mr. Davidson gave up and entertained at the Bismarck. The honeymoon was partly spent at Niagara Falls.

FAR LEFT: Walter Davidson.

LEFT: This is an article about Walter Davidson getting married that was printed in the *Wisconsin Motorist* in 1910.

RIGHT: Gordon Davidson and Doris Burdick's engagement announced.

FAR RIGHT: Gordon and Doris exchange wedding vows in 1934.

"My mother and father were high school sweethearts. They each went away to different colleges. When they both graduated and moved back home, they got married in a ceremony out at Pewaukee Lake. My mother always said that her marriage was a fairy tale come true. She claimed to have had a crush on my dad since grade school." ✹ JD

"My grandmother's last name started with a B and my grandfather's last name started with a D. This simple fact put them in close proximity throughout grade school because of alphabetical seating. A simple coincidence brought my grandparents together. My grandmother also started a family tradition of attending the University of Wisconsin at Madison that still continues in our family today." ▢ JDO

Jean Davidson Is Married

STANDARDS OF pale pink flowers decorated Wauwatosa Congregational Church for the wedding there Saturday of Jean Ellen Davidson and John Howard Oeflein. The couple greeted their friends later at a reception in the gardens of the Wisconsin Club.

The bride is the daughter of Mr. and Mrs. Gordon McLay Davidson, Washington Circle, and the bridegroom's parents are Mrs. Mildred Oeflein, Wauwatosa Avenue, and Milton Oeflein, Hartford.

For the 8 p.m. ceremony, the bride chose a white lace gown. The scalloped neckline of the Empire bodice was detailed with sequins and a bow accented the back of the skirt which fell to a train. A pearl circlet caught her veil and her flowers were stephanotis and orchids.

Her attendants were in lavender organza dresses embroidered in pink and accented with lavender satin cummerbunds. They wore matching net picture hats and carried pink carnations.

Mrs. Alan Baumann of Sault Saint Marie, Mich., was her sister's matron of honor and another sister, Christine Davidson, was bridesmaid with Jean Ende and Mrs. Harold Vandenberg Jr. Patty Glaeser was flower girl in a pink organdy frock.

Robert Oeflein was best man for his brother and ushering were John Joiner, Dallas, Texas, Pat Hassett, Ward Glaeser and Mr. Baumann. Peter Glaeser was ring bearer.

On their return from a trip to Michigan, the couple will make their home on Pewaukee Lake. After Aug. 1, they will reside in Appleton where the bride will complete her studies at Lawrence College.

MRS. JOHN HOWARD OEFLEIN IN HER WEDDING GOWN
The bride is the former Jean Ellen Davidson

B. Artin Haig photo.

ABOVE: Jean Davidson and her mother, Doris.

LEFT: Jean Davidson's sister Barbara helps her get ready.

FAR LEFT: Newspaper article that ran in the *Milwaukee Journal* in 1959.

"My father got a little nervous when he realized how big of a deal his wedding had become. He even asked my grandfather Gordon if they could just have a small ceremony or even elope. Because all the invites had already gone out and the arrangements had been made, Gordon simply told my dad, 'Sorry, kid, but this baby is a done deal.'" ◪ JDO

Jean and John head to the reception.

"We honeymooned across Lake Michigan at a small cottage that was in John's family. It just so happened that my good friend Patty got married on the same day as me. And it just so happened that she and her new husband spent their wedding night at the same hotel as us. To my surprise, she ended up at the table next to me at breakfast! As it turned out they were also taking the ferry to Michigan so we invited them to stay with us at the cottage. The guys fished, and Patty and I tried to cook!" ❋ JD

Best friends of the groom at the Davidson and Oeflein wedding. That is Willie G. Davidson second from the right.

The *Andrea Doria* sinking in 1956.

"In its day, the *Andrea Doria* was considered the most elaborate ocean liner on the seas. It was very prestigious for someone to sail on her, so, of course, my great-grandmother had to go. On the way back from Europe a terrible accident happened. In a thick fog the MS *Stockholm* rammed into her causing extreme damage and the ship started sinking. The crew and passengers went into panic mode. Grandmother Davidson, who was 73 years old, got out of her bunk room and crawled through the smoke to the deck, which was at a 45-degree angle. She sat down and slid across the deck to the rail, then grabbed a rope and slid down it to a waiting rescue boat! She was one of the last survivors to get off the ship before it sank." ▢ JDO

"The rescue boat didn't take her to the pier where the other survivors were, but rather to a navy pier. My father heard of the accident and immediately boarded a plane and flew to New York. He was taken to the main area where the survivors were being cared for and searched in vain for his mother. He was about to call home and inform the family that things didn't look good when a ship steward informed him that some survivors were at another pier. He rushed over and there at the end of the pier was his mother. He ran over to her and all she said was, 'Where the hell have you been?' That was my grandmother. She was indeed the oldest daughter of a bar owner when she married my grandfather, Walter Davidson, in 1910. We all thought she would stop traveling when this happened since she was 73 years old, but we were wrong. She kept right on with her adventures to faraway places!" ✸ JD

OPPOSITE: Walter Davidson's widow, Emma, and Harriet Jacobus, another woman of society, toast Emma's survival of the sinking of the *Andrea Doria* while attending Jean's wedding.

CHAPTER 8

FAMILY DEALERSHIP

Tuesday, June 17, 1969

Moto~~rcycle~~ Outlet Sold

George A. Knuth, who has been selling Harley-Davidson motorcycles in Milwaukee county for nearly four decades, has sold his franchise to the son-in-law of a member of the Davidson family.

The county franchise for Harley-Davidson motorcycles now is owned by John Oeflein, 35, Elm Grove. His wife, Jean, is the daughter of the late Gordon Davidson, who was vice-president of manufacturing for the Harley-Davidson Motor Co. Oeflein's company is Mil-

Knuth   **Oeflein**

waukee Harley-Davidson, Inc. He operates two outlets — at 6312 W. Fond du Lac av. and 1753 S. Muskego av. The former is a new location; the latter was the south side store for the Knuth Co. In addition to the motorcycles, Oeflein also will sell a line of Arctic Cat snowmobiles.

The Knuth Co., 2491 W. Fond du Lac av., will continue in business but will not sell motorcycles. It will have a five county dealership — Milwaukee, Waukesha, Ozaukee, Washington and Sheboygan — for a line of Harley-Davidson utility vehicles and golf carts.

"When my father married my mother, he worked as a salesman for the General Cable Company. It wasn't until a few years later that he got involved with the family business. He was flying to the Indianapolis 500 with Walter C. Davidson, who was the Motor Company's vice president of sales and was in charge of the dealerships. He asked my dad if he liked his job, because there was an upcoming opportunity for a dealership and it was right in Milwaukee. Walter made a deal with my dad. He said that a motorcycle would be waiting for him at the factory. He was supposed to pick it up and ride it all the way to Florida. Walter said, 'Take your time and stop at every dealership on the way. I don't want to see you back here for a month! When you do get back, we will talk business if you are still interested.' My dad packed his saddlebags, kissed my mom goodbye and was off. He had a great trip and even met up with Willie G. Davidson at the bike races in Daytona Beach. He and Willie G. were high school buddies and they always had fun together. When my dad finally got back to Milwaukee, he called Walter and said, 'Where do I sign?'" JDO

"When my husband went on his adventure, I was jealous because I had just had our fourth child and thought to myself, 'He looks like Marlon Brando going off on a fun-filled holiday and I am home changing diapers!'" JD

An article that ran in the *Milwaukee Journal.*

Jon, William and Lori Oeflein at the construction site of their parents' new Milwaukee Harley-Davidson dealership.

"The Milwaukee area had been serviced by dealer Bill Knuth for decades. He is a legend in the motorcycle world. He opened the Knuth Cycle Company in 1925. He had been a top salesman for an outfit selling Indians right in Milwaukee, but switched to Harley-Davidsons when he opened his own shop. There is no doubt in my mind that a certain Arthur Davidson had a hand in the brand switch! He remained an H-D dealer until the day he died. Knuth was a large guy with a warm personality. He was a driving force behind the promotion of the Motor Company during the good years and the bad. My husband had some big shoes to fill, so it was good that he was young and full of energy." ❀ JD

"I have great memories of working for my dad in the parts department. This was pre-computer times, so there was a huge set of parts books. I quickly learned the easy and most often requested parts, like turn signal bulbs or spark plugs, but I was still learning about motors and transmissions. Many times big bikers would come in with a need of a set of oversized rings or a valve seat or something, and they could tell that this skinny kid had no idea what they were talking about. They would say, 'Maybe you should get your dad,' but I would say, 'Maybe you could help me find it'. With this I would turn the books around and let them take over the search. They always seemed to enjoy this and I got valuable lessons on what goes on inside a motor. If neither of us could find the right part, then I would have to yell, 'Dad!'" ▨ JDO

"Part of my duties as a kid working in the parts department was to uncrate the new bikes when they were delivered. It was always fun breaking open the crates and seeing the shiny, new Milwaukee Iron. One day in late summer, while I was out in the back parking lot uncrating the new bikes, it became time to perform one of my other duties. This was to shag lunch for everyone. I would walk through the office, the sales floor and finally down the mechanic's row to make a list. We would usually go to Captain's Burger Stand, which was right down the street. On my way back, I noticed two guys trying to load a new Sportster into the back of their van! I couldn't believe my eyes. I dropped the lunch and started yelling for the mechanics, Steve and Pineapple. The hoodlums jumped in their van and took off. Too bad for them that when they made the turn into the alley, the Sporty slid out onto the pavement still sitting on the bottom pallet of the crate! I ran over to it and to my surprise, it didn't have a scratch on it. By now the mechanics were outside, and my dad ran out shortly after. To the guys I was a hero, except for the fact that I dropped their lunch. My dad, on the other hand, was not so happy. He told me that I meant much more to him than any motorcycle. 'Things,' he said, 'could be replaced,' but he could never replace me." 🖼 JDO

The new bikes get delivered to the back of the northside shop.

"Everyone liked my dad. He treated everyone as an equal. It didn't matter if it was a guy restoring a ratty old Sportster on a shoestring budget or a wealthy fellow buying a brand-new full-dresser, they got the same good service. They called my dad Captain Johnny and many regulars called me Captain Jonny Jr. I liked this and it made me feel good to be compared to my dad, who seemed to know everything." JDO

Milwaukee Harley-Davidson interior in the early 1970s.

RIGHT: Lori riding her horse, Diane.

BELOW: Jon, Sue and William, at a horse show in the early 1970s.

"I didn't spend much time at the dealership. I had finally got my dream farm in the country and was busy training and showing our horses. I also was busy with five children!" ✸ JD

LEFT: Peter wins his first horse show trophy.

BELOW: Susan smiles big while sitting on Pandora.

FAR LEFT: John Oeflein cleans the windshield on a Harley-Davidson snowmobile so his children, William and Susan, can get back to the fun.

LEFT: John Oeflein with children Susan and Peter on a Kitty Cat, which was a small snowmobile made by Arctic Cat.

"We handled not only motorcycles, but snowmobiles as well. We had the H-Ds and also the full line from Arctic Cat. When we would head up to northern Wisconsin on snowmobile trips, my dad would haul a huge trailer loaded with five to six machines. I am sorry to say that when it was time to ride, everyone scrambled for the Arctic Cats. The H-D snowmobile was a first-generation model and needed to be refined, but it was a short-lived venture." ▣ JDO

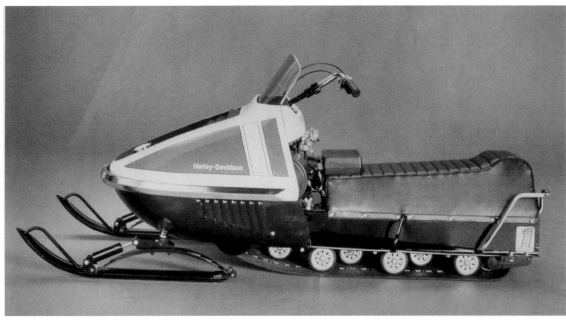

LEFT: Promotional picture of the Harley-Davidson snowmobile, 1972.

OPPOSITE: Miss Wisconsin 1973, Judy Hieke, poses with the new Arctic Cat Cheetah model.

"One day in the summer of 1976 a really nice farmer named Ray Klinger came into our dealership. He was riding a 1940 Harley-Davidson EL, which he had purchased brand-new. He said that he trades in every 35 years and this was the year! He then asked my dad if he was interested in taking in an old bike that had always run great. Ray also added that two other dealers had already turned him down, so he would understand if no one wanted his old bike even though he swore that he had always taken extra good care of it and that it had its own stall in his barn! My dad was glad to inform Ray that he loved old bikes and that he would give him a brand-new 1977 Super Glide in a straight-up trade. Old Ray was so happy he could barely contain himself." ▨ JDO

Ray Klinger of Hartford, Wisconsin, trades his 1940 Model EL (61" Knucklehead) on a 1977 Model FXE Superglide. Ray told John Oeflein of Milwaukee Harley-Davidson that he "trades every 35 years." His EL runs like new with 38,000 miles on it.

Susan Davidson Lee in 2008.

An article from the *Milwaukee Journal* in 1976.

**William McLay Oeflein
and his wife, Petique.**

"Everyone in the family loves to ride Old Ray's Knucklehead." JDO

A promotional picture from H-D showing the fun side of motorcycles.

Dear Sir,

Does Harley make a bike under 200 cc espeually for long trips on the high-way that a girl 5'3" 110 lbs could handle? About how much would it set me back? I'm running away and cant afford much — but then again I have a rich father. Please send me some Harley Books ok?

Kathy Kopca
423 Gruenhagen Hall
Oshkosh, Wis.
54901

Actual letter sent to the Milwaukee Harley-Davidson dealership.

RAISED on TWO WHEELS

Founder Walter Davidson and his son, Gordon. in August 1923.

"My grandfather rode his motorcycle every day to and from work. Even in the winter. The Motor Company was a pioneer when it came to cold weather riding gear." ⧄ JDO

"When I was a little girl, I always rode in the sidecar, but sometimes my mom and sister wanted to go too. That is when I got the best seat because I got to ride right behind my dad. It was great fun and I felt very special. I couldn't see around him, so I would just hold on tight, especially when we hit the bumps!" ✳ JD

ABOVE: Gordon Davidson gets a warm welcome home from daughter Barbara.

LEFT: Gordon Davidson with daughter, Jean, in the sidecar in 1940.

LEFT: Peter Oeflein getting a ride in on a chilly fall day.

BELOW: A picture captured from home movies of John Oeflein with his son, Jon.

"I have great memories of riding around in front of my dad when I was really little. We lived in the city at that time, so when my dad got home from the shop, he would plop me down in front of him and we would just loop around the house. When we grew a little older, my dad set up a track around the yard with a few small jumps. All the neighborhood kids would be over, and we would have races with three or four going at a time. There were a lot of crashes, but the kids always came back for more! It was definitely way before today's legal climate." ◼ JDO

John Oeflein with his children, Peter, Susan and William McLay, in 1977.

"John and I found a beautiful piece of property out in the country. The house dated back to the Civil War and there were barns for our horses!" ✸ JD

"We now had lots of room to ride motorcycles every day. We made trails everywhere and built a full-size motocross track for my brother, William! My little brother has a great historical name. Not only is he another William in the Davidson and Harley tradition, but his middle name is McLay after the hermit uncle that lent the original founders of the Motor Company the seed money to get the whole thing started." ▨ JDO

"Everyone loves Harley-Davidson T-shirts. In fact, whenever I see one I smile a little inside. It makes me proud that my family started something that has become a part of the culture of the world. Well, my pals in high school loved H-D shirts with a passion and they all knew where to get them—in my dresser! Every kid that came over usually left with a new shirt. One time my dad came home just as I was leaving with some friends. He stopped one of the kids and asked him if he had gained weight. He then proceeded to examine the kid's wardrobe and he discovered the kid had six H-D shirts on under his own shirt! We had him leave five of the shirts, but, of course, my dad sent him home with one. My dad used to joke that all the parents of the kids at my school should thank him for dressing their kids!" ▨ JDO

LEFT: Jon at the wheel of his dune buggy with a friend in 1976.

BELOW: 1976 AMF Roadmaster moped.

"Country life was fun—but I really wanted to get to Big Cedar Lake because all my pals hung out there. My friend Dan Giove lived on the east side of the lake and I would sometimes ride my bicycle to his cottage, but it was close to 15 miles. I already knew how to drive everything from tractors to cars, but I couldn't take anything on the street. Many days I felt trapped. Then one day in the mid-1970s my dad brought home an AMF Roadmaster moped prototype. It was about the coolest thing I had ever seen! It resembled a small motorcycle, but it had pedals. My dad said I could drive it anywhere, but I needed to take notes how it ran for the company, since it was still in development. He then added that if I saw a cop I should shut off the little gas motor and pedal! I was finally free! With a top speed of nearly 30 miles per hour, I rode that thing everywhere. It must have been how my great-grandfather Walter felt when he went off to the lakes on the first Harley-Davidson—an incredible feeling of freedom. I wore the tires off that little moped, and every time I passed a cop I just pedaled. You should have seen the look on one cop's face when I went past him going 30 miles per hour, up a hill, and barely pedaling! I turned in notes every now and then, but I later found them in my dad's desk drawer. I think my dad just said that to make me feel important, which I did." JDO

BELOW: 1960 Harley-Davidson Topper equipped with a 165cc single-cylinder two-stroke engine.

"People don't think about small H-D motorcycles these days, but over the years the company made many different types and styles of lightweight machines. The unique Topper scooter was made from 1960 to 1965. It had a fully enclosed engine compartment and is started with a rope pull, like a lawn mower!" ◈ JDO

HD–27893

1968 Harley-Davidson Rapido. This nifty little bike had a 125cc engine and was quite popular.

"When I finally turned 16 and got my driver's license, my dad brought me home a brand-new Sportster! I was the happiest kid on the planet! I think he really liked to spoil us. Well, I rode to high school every day and was having the time of my life until a Friday in late May. I ditched out of school at lunch on my new bike with a particularly cute girl on the back. We rode out to the lakes and then back to town to meet up with my other riding pals after school. When we got back, all the students were out in front waiting for their buses. Instead of pulling in, I decided to hammer it and blow by the school, getting up to about 85-90 miles per hour! All the kids were cheering and I thought I was pretty cool. Well, what I didn't realize was a cop had been trying to pull me over for a mile or so before we got to school and now was in hot pursuit with siren on and red lights flashing right behind me! The Sportster had been retrofitted with straight pipes and they were super-loud. I never heard the copper, but he, and the entire school, thought I was trying to outrun him! When I finally got to a stop sign, three squads came from all directions and the ride was over. I ended up getting four different citations in that one incident and that was how I lost my driver's license the first time." ■ JDO

**1980 Harley-Davidson
XLH-1000.**

**Jon Davidson Oeflein
and David Berth
enjoying a summer
motorcycle outing.**

"When I was young, I was not the cautious type. Many things happened on two wheels, including an incident that I will never forget. It happened one morning on my way to Madison. I was headed to sign up for classes at the University of Wisconsin for my junior year and was running late as usual. It was really early in the morning and I was racing up and down the hills on a country road. The fog was thick in the valleys, but would clear as you went up the hill on the other side. It was quite fun; however, the visibility kept going from good to terrible to good again. Well, as I crested one hill and raced down into the fog in the next valley, a wall of black and white appeared that blocked the entire road! It seems that a farmer was moving his heard of milkers from their current pasture to one on the other side of the road, which is a quite common thing in the dairy state of Wisconsin. I only had a split second to react, so I didn't brake, but rather aimed for a tiny gap between two cows and kept on the gas. My short life flashed before my eyes, but somehow I went shooting right through! When I stopped on the top of the next hill, I noticed black cow hair stuck to my brake and clutch levers! Considering that dairy cows are about the size of a small car, I think my great-grandfather Walter must have been looking out for me." ▨ JDO

"During my college years at University of Wisconsin at Madison, I would always try to get over to the football stadium and see my relatives. My Grandmother Davidson had an area of the parking lot reserved for everyone to tailgate party before the game. I always had some motorcycle at school with me, usually a trade-in or a demo bike. Well, it so happens that the only bike my dad would let me take that week was a used Kawasaki. When Saturday game day came, I rode over to the parking lot to visit with all my Davidson relatives. I really didn't even think twice about the brand of motorcycle I was on. As soon as I parked, one of my cousins had some choice words for me! I quickly grabbed a blanket from the trunk of my grandmother's Cadillac (she liked Caddys, but my grandfather was a Chevy man) and threw it over the foreign bike!" ▨ JDO

Jon on a Harley-Davidson FXR stopped on Wells Street in downtown Milwaukee in 1982.

Lori on her Harley-Davidson "California Sport Glide" in 1980.

"One time she rode her bike over to a boyfriend's house and was parking it in his driveway. It was on a bit of a slant and she almost tipped her big bike over. Much to her dismay, the boyfriend was watching her and just stood there and laughed. He told her if she was going to ride it she better be able to pick it up! The next week Lori asked if she could go on a motorcycle trip out West with this boyfriend. I never thought to say no for a second. I guess because I was raised with such freedom. They went and I remember other parents saying I was nuts. Thank goodness they had a wonderful adventure all over the West." ❀ JD

Road trip.

"My eldest daughter, Lori, worked at our dealership during the summers when she was in high school. She remembers sneaking into her father's office to watch *The Days of Our Lives* soap on the small television in the corner. She always thought no one knew until one day her father asked her on the way home, 'So what happened in today's episode?'" ❀ JD

"Customers would come into our dealership and see my sister working and ask me, 'Who's the cutie?' and I would respond with, 'That's my sister!' She also really liked a particular Electra Glide that had been set up 'Cali-style' (no fairing, etc.) and would take it home on a regular basis, even though she barely weighed a hundred pounds!" ❖ JDO

The happy family rides together! Jon and Kristi with sons, Nic and Carter, in the sidehack in 2003.

"My family has long tradition of attending the University of Wisconsin at Madison. My mother, my sister Barbara, as well as myself and John all attended this great school. Then son Jon and daughters, Lori and Susan, and my daughter-in-law Kristi graced the halls in Madison. I am now proud to say that my grandson, Nicolas Davidson Oeflein, is going to continue the tradition. It is a great school and many say that the first Harley-Davidson motor designs were drawn up in the engineering department when founder William S. Harley was attending. His professors might have helped with the designs, or maybe it was Harley teaching his professors!" ❂ JD

ABOVE: Jon Davidson Oeflein with his father.

ABOVE: Jean rides in the sidecar with husband John. Their two sons, Jon (driving) and Peter, join on this ride.

LEFT: Jon's son, Carter, dreaming about taking one of dad's Panheads for a spin.

OPPOSITE: Peter Oeflein sits on his 1950 Harley-Davidson FL.

CHAPTER 10

EVEL

ABOVE: Evel's customized Harley-Davidson XR-750.

LEFT: Evel Knievel speaks to the large crowd before his jump.

"In 1971 Evel Knievel came to Chicago, IL, to do one of his motorcycle jumps. On the way to the event, I was thinking he was reckless and I remember telling our children that he must not be very smart to put himself in such danger. But when we arrived and spent some time hanging out with him, I kind of changed my mind. We were his special guests and he was really friendly and took what he did very seriously. I had a new view of him; however, I still did not want my children to grow up to be stunt performers!" ❋ JD

"I was just a kid when we all went down to see Evel jump. I remember it was very exciting and the atmosphere was electric. We got the V.I.P. treatment and front-row seating. It was really exciting! " ▢ JDO

Willie G. Davidson (center) waits for the action to start.

RIGHT: Jean Davidson with daughter, Lori, and son, Jon. Nancy Davidson, Willie G.'s wife, is in the background with their children.

"Before the jump, Evel invited us to hang out with him in his trailer. He was really nice and was dressing for his stunt. He was only wearing a small red, white and blue towel the whole time we were with him. I noticed a scar on his arm and asked him about it. This got him going and he proceeded to tell us that he had broken every major bone in his body! He then started showing us scar after scar and detailing what jump he had gotten them from. I was mesmerized by this stuntman. He was the real deal." ◼ JDO

LEFT: (Left to right) Lori and Jon Oeflein, Michael, Bill and Karen Davidson, and William Oeflein.

OPPOSITE: Evel in action.

"When Evel jumped that day in Chicago, I could not believe that a guy on a motorcycle could fly through the air over that many cars. When it was time to jump, he had to start from the hallway and zoom through a propped-open door to get enough speed, and then he had to speed through another door after he landed before he came to a stop in another hallway!" ❀ JD

"He warmed up the crowd by doing huge wheelies back and forth in the indoor arena. Exhaust and smoke filled the huge venue, setting the stage for the big jump! One of the most remarkable things I remember was at the peak of Evel's jump. I swear his head was no more than a foot or two from the steel girders! I think back about this and wonder if this was carefully planned or if he had just kind of winged it!" ▢ JDO

A time lapse of Evel jumping semi tractors outdoors.

"Evel and I were invited to the grand opening of Buddy Stubbs' new museum at his dealership. The museum houses Buddy's private collection of motorcycles. It was really fun spending time with Evel and talking about old times. I also was honored to be with my good friend, Buddy, for this special event. I was very worried about Evel's health, especially after he needed to be taken to the hospital during the event. But, proving that he was one tough guy, even this didn't stop him, and sure enough he was back at the event the very next morning. Unfortunately, this was one of Evel's last public appearances." ❀ JD

"Evel Knievel was truly a daredevil and lived on the edge. I am not sure the world will see too many more guys like him. I am proud to say I knew him and was able to see him perform." ▧ JDO

"One time Evel came to our dealership and offered to perform a jump to promote our business. I can't remember why it never panned out, but I do remember that he wanted $25K and it had to be in cash and paid before the jump!" ❀ JD

Evel Knievel (left), Jean Davidson and Buddy Stubbs at Buddy Stubbs' Harley-Davidson in Phoenix, AZ.

"Evel Knievel was so big in his era that a movie was made about his life. In 1971 popular actor George Hamilton played Evel in the film that documented his life. They used lots of actual footage of Evel's jumps in the movie, and Evel himself performed several new jumps just for the production. These new jumps included an incredible leap of 129 feet over 19 cars that set the world record!" 🔲 JDO

ABOVE: Actor George Hamilton and actress Sue Lyon.

LEFT: Actor George Hamilton as Evel Knievel.

CHAPTER 11

FUN and GAMES

"Slim Cole was a stuntman and actor who appeared in old silent westerns and serials in the 1920s and 1930s. He loved motorcycles and was famous for racing his bike at high speeds over the Cahuenga Pass near Universal Studios in California. Supposedly he also broke the nose of legendary producer Sam Warner in a heated argument." ✉ JDO

Stuntman Slim Cole.

"Motorcycles were quite novel in the early days and were often used to entertain audiences between horse races or at county fairs." ✷ JD

"People love to get together and have fun. Motorcycle clubs found great ways to compete on their bikes at slow speeds as to avoid any serious injuries at a social event, and, of course, there was beer involved." ✷ JD

"One of the most popular events is riding the planks. Boards are laid down in a line and a rider must start from a dead stop at one end and see how many boards he can ride across without falling off. It makes for lots of laughs." ▣ JDO

LEFT: Riding the planks back in the day.

BELOW: Jon Davidson Oeflein riding the planks at the Harley-Davidson Museum in 2012.

OPPOSITE: Early western show that used a Harley-Davidson.

"My favorite fun event is the blindfold race. It is for couples only and the man has to wear a blindfold while he drives! The woman rides along and has to tell her man how to navigate through the course. It is very entertaining and usually leads to a crash or two. It is always set up in a large grassy area for obvious reasons. The part of this contest I like best is that the woman is in complete control!" ❀ JD

The famous blindfold race in the 1940s.

**A young rider
perfecting his stunts.**

**Kathleen Karr and
Bebe Stanton, two
New York actresses,
pose on a Harley-
Davidson in 1927.**

**Club members help out
after a picnic mishap.**

"After WWII the guys that rode H-Ds in the service continued riding them back home. These war era bikes are popular with today's collectors." JDO

**BELOW: Bill and Diane
Rodencal on a 1942
WLA in 2012.**

"Social clubs have always been a part of motorcycling." ✸ JD

CHAPTER 12

RACING

An early Harley-Davidson Pocket Valve burns around the dirt track.

"Pretty much as soon as mankind figured how to attach a small combustion motor to a bicycle they were not content just riding around. Of course they had to start to see which motor bike was the fastest. It is just the way the world turns. Harley-Davidson's racing history goes all the way back to 1904. In the early days the motor-driven machines were just a sideshow at intermission or after the horse races." ▣ JDO

"My grandfather was a bicycle racer when he was young and actually won several road races in the greater Milwaukee area. This gave him a good foundation of riding skills when he moved to motorcycle racing." ✹ JD

"Many people didn't want motorcycles to participate at any of the race tracks because they often scared the horses." ▣ JDO

"Racing evolved into many different forms and styles. Man on machine against man on machine." JDO

Harley-Davidson team racer sits with a happy smile.

Legendary racer Joe Petrali poses in the saddle before a race.

"My grandfather Walter was an excellent endurance racer. The event is really more of a contest than a race. Each rider starts with 1,000 points and then has to get his machine to a series of checkpoints in accordance with a predetermined schedule. The rider gets points deducted for being too early or too late. Sometimes the contests went on for multiple days." ✳ JD

"I think it was Walter's meticulous nature that enabled him to be so good on endurance runs. Of course his ability to ride a motorcycle and being a crack mechanic didn't hurt either. Many times riders had to fix their machines themselves during the event. Some teams would send chase vehicles along with spare parts and tools, but my great-grandfather was known to go it alone. Both my kid brothers were involved in racing— William in motocross and Peter in motocross and endurance events." ▨ JDO

ABOVE: Merv Molgaard, on his flathead Harley-Davidson, leaves Erv Tursky, on his Indian, in the dust, circa 1940.

LEFT: Racing was dangerous and led to deep bonds between team members.

"My father and I would go to the races whenever we could and I would love to watch the guys fly around the track. It looked so exciting to a young girl. Those were the days when girls had limited options for careers, so all I could do was dream about being a motorcycle racer. When I was a teenager, I thought Joe Leonard was the cutest guy around. On the track I would cheer and cheer for him. It all looked so neat. Then one day some racers came to our home and I heard all the stories of the injuries and the painful accidents that went along with racing. I still thought if I was a boy, I would be a racer just like Joe Leonard." ✳ JD

"Joe Leonard was an aggressive, hard-charging racer. His wild style and fearless attitude led him to become the first champion of the AMA Grand National Series in 1954." ▦ JDO

RIGHT: Joe Leonard was the AMA's first Grand National champion.

OPPOSITE: Flat track action.

HD·24026

"Paul Goldsmith had a short, but very productive
motorcycle racing career before he switched
to car racing. He claimed 27 AMA titles riding
Harley-Davidsons in the early 1950s." ▦ JDO

**RIGHT: Racer Paul
Goldmith.**

**OPPOSITE: Charles
Marshall (third from left)
trackside in the 1950s.**

OPPOSITE: Harley-Davidson factory team racer Cal Rayborn is often called the world's greatest racer.

RIGHT: Walter C. Davidson (second from right) hanging out with the officials at the starting line.

UP and OVER THE TOP

CHAPTER 13

**Herb Reiber poses
on his bike before a
hillclimb event in 1925.**

"The hillclimb is one of the oldest forms of motor-driven machine competition. It started back in France in late 1897 and remains popular today. The object is to race vehicles up a very steep slope. The winner is the person who makes it the furthest up the hill or best yet to the top. If more than one participant makes it to the top, then it is the one that got there the fastest who claims the trophy. On a motorcycle it is not a safe sport and spectacular crashes are the norm." JDO

"The sport is for young men and there is lots of action. The spectators always get a great show, but take it from me, sitting on the hillside is no place for a mother whose sons are participating." JD

"There were many hillclimb events in the Milwaukee area and some still remain. My father would attend many and cheer on the factory riders." ❀ JD

"The Harley-Davidson factory helped out a lot with the hillclimb machines. The motors had to be souped up in order to compete and the racing department loved to experiment. These bikes were called homebrews by the public that had no way of buying one. Bill Knuth sponsored the only dealer team in the country, Knuth's Klimbers." ▦ JDO

Almost to the top.

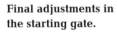

Final adjustments in the starting gate.

"Hillclimb events were very popular in the 1920s and 30s. It was mostly a professional sport and the motorcycles were highly modified. The rear ends were stretched back to help keep the front ends down and prevent the machines from flipping over backward on the steep slope. When this did happen, and it wasn't rare, the only thing a rider could do was to try to get out of the way of the airborne motorcycle!" ▨ JDO

ABOVE: Halfway up the course.

OPPOSITE: Trouble!

CHAPTER 14

THE LAW

"Harley-Davidson has been involved with police departments almost since its inception. The durable and dependable machines made a good addition to a fleet of cars. There are things that can be accomplished much better and more efficiently on a motorcycle." ◈ JDO

ABOVE: Directing traffic in the 1930s.

LEFT: Early policeman working using his Harley-Davidson.

Popular comic that ran in *The Mounted Officer*.

Cover of *The Mounted Officer* publication.

"Harley-Davidson was so dedicated to making motorcycles for law enforcement that they even put out a publication on their behalf." JD

"The publication was around in the 1920s for a while and is now back in publication. The Motor Company remains dedicated to law enforcement around the world." JDO

"We used to share my parents spare cottage on Pewaukee Lake with my sister Barbara and her family. One time my children and I were driving out there kind of late at night. Suddenly there was a police motorcycle right behind us with its lights on and siren blasting! I remember I was speeding a little and thought, 'Oh, darn!' I quickly pulled over and the bike cop was right behind me. He then used a megaphone and proceeded to tell me to get out of the car and that I was under arrest! I hopped out in shock only to see my husband was the cop! He laughed and laughed!" ❀ JD

"I will never forget when my dad pulled this stunt. Me and my brothers' and sisters' eyes were as big as dinner plates while we watched from the car. But the joke ended up on my dad as it just so happened that a real policeman drove past the fake arrest scene and became suspicious. He followed us all home and then pulled in the cottage with his real red lights flashing. My dad almost got a big ticket for impersonating a police officer! However, the real cop used to be a bike cop and remembered my dad from the dealership and let him off." ▦ JDO

HARLEY-DAVIDSON POLICE MODEL

★

RADIO equipped

The Harley-Davidson police motorcycle radio offered for 1936 is the result of intensive development and is proving its dependability and efficiency in scores of departments throughout the nation. The entire set, convertor, antenna and speaker, is designed to function as a synchronized unit. It is Harley-Davidson designed and built for exclusive use on Harley-Davidson police motorcycles. The finest, strongest built set on the market!

The Modern Mounted Minute Man

LEFT: A well-outfitted police model Servi-Car in the 1960s.

OPPOSITE: Longtime Harley-Davidson employee Charles "Dick" Marshall shows off the new 1949 FL before it gets outfitted with police gear.

Jon Davidson Oeflein sits on right, with his brother William on the far left and a family friend in the middle. They are waiting for the parade to start in 1968.

"My dad always liked to bring a bike home to ride in the area parades. It was really fun as a kid to ride on the back while he turned on the siren and the lights. Everyone got a big kick out of it." ▨ JDO

ABOVE: John driving a police-outfitted motorcycle with daughter, Lori, and son, Jon, riding on the box in the Elm Grove Memorial Day Parade.

OPPOSITE: Story that appeared in the *Milwaukee Journal* in 1982.

Milwaukee, WI 53202

JOURNAL   Tuesday, June 22, 1982   Part 2

—*Journal Photo*

HARLEY SALE — Dealer John Oeflein of Harley-Davidson of Milwaukee, which is located at 6312 Fond du Lac Ave., led Milwaukee Police Sgt. Ralph Junge on a tour of inspection of 10 Harley-Davidson motorcycles that the police department took delivery of Monday.

Harley dealership owner kept police on wheels

Oeflein married into Davidson family

By AMY RABIDEAU SILVERS
asilvers@journalsentinel.com

John Oeflein didn't even know how much he liked motorcycles until he married into a family named Davidson.

That, of course, is Davidson as in Harley-Davidson.

Ten years later, Oeflein bought a dealership, Milwaukee Harley-Davidson Inc., and consolidated the Milwaukee County franchise on N. Fond du Lac Ave.

"He ran it for 24 years, supplying all the Milwaukee Police Department motorcycles," said son Jon Oeflein. "It was always a big deal when the new bikes came in every year and the cops came in to get their bikes. And the dealership serviced everything for the Police Department, too."

Oeflein died of prostate can-

cer Feb. 5 while wintering in Hobe Sound, Fla. He was 72. He was a longtime resident of Elm Grove, last living in Jackson in Washington County.

He grew up in Wauwatosa,  where he was friends with an older daughter in the Davidson family. Later, while at the University of Wisconsin-Madison, he began dating Jean Davidson, a younger daughter.

Oeflein

Oeflein graduated with a bachelor's degree in the light building industry.

"My dad started in sales in Chicago, working for General Cable — I think they made different wires and cables — and then worked mostly in Milwaukee," Jon said.

He and Jean Davidson married in 1959, and became the par-

OBITUARY

ents of five children.

Her grandfather, Walter Davidson, was a founder and the first president of Harley-Davidson. Her father was Gordon Davidson, vice president of manufacturing with the company. An uncle, Walter C. Davidson, vice president in charge of sales, suggested that Oeflein purchase the dealership when it became available.

Custom orders would include special-use motorcycles for police departments.

"They made a three-wheeled vehicle — called the Servicar — for parking checkers," Jon said. "And regular bikes for pursuit and patrol."

The dealership was, Jon said, a fascinating place for a boy to grow up. A steady stream of burly motorcycle cops would come in for service and equipment, looking pretty impressive in their bike leathers.

"They called my dad 'Captain John,' " he said. "I'd be hanging around in the shop, having an orange pop on Saturday. I remember them picking me up like I was a feather and plopping me on the counter, calling me 'Captain Johnny Jr.' "

His father, who was interested in old cars as a young man, began collecting antique motorcycles and boats and more cars.

The couple divorced in 1981. The dealership was sold in 1985.

"He was very funny, witty, almost sarcastic," Jon said. "He'd figure you out — he was intuitive — and he made you laugh."

Other survivors include daughters Lori Walker and Susan Lee; sons William and Peter; sister Mary Jane Joiner; and grandchildren.

A memorial gathering will be held, beginning with visitation at 2 p.m. Saturday at St. John's Lutheran Church, 2881 Division Road, Jackson. A service will follow at 3 p.m.

Story that appeared in the *Milwaukee Journal* in 2006.

ON the LIGHTER SIDE

CHAPTER 15

"Bailey's H-D dealership in Fort Wayne, IN, brought me in for a book signing. I gave a presentation and then even got a kiss from the HOG! I love how creative the dealers get in order to have their customers enjoy themselves." ❁ JD

Jean kissing the HOG.

Dick Klaesing with his Harley Hopeful.

ABOVE:
Chill Out Chapter

Jean Davidson with biker who had her sign his head.

The H-D founders tattooed on biker's back.

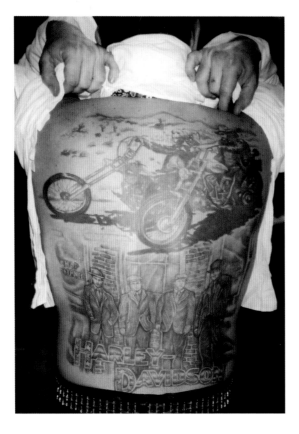

"Wherever I travel around the world, I am always amazed by the tattoos that people love to show me. They really are works of art and I always ask what the story is that goes with each one. One guy had the four H-D founders across his back. I wonder what they would think about having their pictures on someone's back. Would they be honored or think it was silly? They never thought of themselves as anyone special. They just wanted to make the best motorcycles." ❀ JD

"I was doing a book signing out in Las Vegas and a man asked me to sign his head. I laughed and said, 'Sure.' The next day he came back and said he went to a high power meeting and couldn't get the signature off! We both laughed, until he realized he had meetings for the next three days!" ❀ JD

"When I was in Hungary for the largest European motorcycle rally, a man came up to me and asked me to sign his body. I said sure and with that he dropped his pants. My daughter just stood there and laughed. Sure enough I signed his lower abdomen. He left smiling and the next day he came back and dropped his pants again to show me my name tattooed! That was and is my most unusual signing that I have ever done." ❀ JD

"Motorcycles got a bit of a bad reputation after Hollywood released a series of biker gang movies. The Motor Company then spent years trying to lighten up its image." ⊠ JDO

LEFT: Jim Bambard with his 1948 Harley-Davidson M-125.

CELEBRATE HARLEY-DAVIDSON

CHAPTER 16

"It was my pleasure to have a longtime relationship with my father's cousin, Arthur Harley Davidson. Since my dad died when I was in my 20s, Arthur became my surrogate father and I always called him Uncle Arthur. I looked to him for advice and he loved to give it. He liked to help with my books. When people told me stories about Harley-Davidson history that I hadn't heard before, I would run out to his home and ask him if this really happened. Even if it meant going to his winter home in the Virgin Islands! He passed away at 97 years old and I miss him every day." ✻ JD

ABOVE LEFT: Jean Davidson with Arthur Harley Davidson.

ABOVE: (Left to right) Steven and Susan Lee, Jean Davidson, Arthur Harley Davidson, Kristi and Jon Oeflein with Nicolas and Carter Oeflein in the front row at the 100th anniversary of H-D celebration.

TOP: (Left to right) Jean Davidson, Mary Harley Stocking and Sarah Harley O'Hearn planning a party for all the Harley and Davidson descendents in 2003.

BOTTOM: William Godfrey Davidson, who is known all over the world as simply Willie G.

"People love Willie G. because he is always friendly and greets each and every one of them. I grew up calling him Uncle Bill, even though he and my mom are actually cousins. I have such great memories of doing lots of fun stuff with him and his family. He has done so much for the Motor Company that it is hard to even comprehend." ▨ JDO

"When my New York friends, Ernie and Mary, came to Milwaukee, of course I took them to the H-D museum. They were thrilled to have their picture taken with my cousin Willie G. and his wife, Nancy. Whenever friends from around the world come to visit, we all go down to the museum. Everyone always loves it." ✳ JD

(Left to right) Ernie and Mary Barkman from Athens, New York. Willie G. and Nancy Davidson and Jean Davidson at the Harley-Davidson Museum.

"We all gathered for a rally in Milwaukee. My
first book, *Growing Up Harley-Davidson*, had just
been released. It was a really exciting time." ✸ JD

LEFT: Willie G. and
his wife, Nancy,
standing in front of a
reproduction of the
famous shed where it
all began.

ABOVE: (Left to right) Willie
G. Davidson, Kathy Davidson
Bruce, Lori Walker, Jean
Davidson, Karen Davidson,
Nancy Davidson and Michael
Davidson in September 2001.

"I am always honored to be asked to be the Grand Marshal of a parade. The antique motorcycle parade for the 100-year celebration of Harley-Davidson was especially fun. What an honor to ride through the countryside and see so many people out waving as we came by with this long line of old motorcycles." ❁ JD

"It was cool seeing my mom as the Grand Marshal of the Fourth of July parade in her home town of Wauwatosa, WI." ▫ JDO

ABOVE: Jean Davidson as Grand Marshal for a Fourth of July parade.

LEFT: Jean Davidson in sidecar of a 1915 H-D being driven by longtime friend Bob Jameson. John Harley rides behind.

OPPOSITE: (Left to right) Dan Henke, Jean Davidson, Peter Oeflein, Don Dzurick, Jon Davidson Oeflein, Brian Kohlman and Kevin Griffith at the 100-year anniversary of Walter Davidson's 1908 endurance race victory in Catskill, NY, in 2008.

"What a thrill to be invited to be the speaker at the 100-year anniversary of the famous Catskill endurance race that my grandfather won in 1908. I was honored to lead the parade down the main street that my grandfather rode a century earlier." ✱ JD

ABOVE: Ernie Barkman drives Jean Davidson in the front of the parade down the main street in Catskill, NY. Jon is riding on their right with family friend, Tony Jankoski, following close behind.

"My good friend Buddy Stubbs owns two Harley-Davidson dealerships in Arizona. He has a long history with H-D, going back to when his father owned a dealership in Illinois. He has done things with motorcycles that most people only dream of. From racer to Hollywood stuntman, he has done it all." ❀ JD

Buddy Stubbs with his parents Carl and Corky Stubbs in 1941.

**Buddy Stubbs and Jean
at a ride to benefit the
Davidson Yell and Tell
charity, in Arizona
in 2010.**

"Buddy told me a story about when he was 13 back in 1953: 'Me and my father would make the trip to Milwaukee with our pickup truck. We were only picking up one Servi-Car for the Decatur Police Department. We filled the bed of the pickup with parts and decided we would ride the trike back to Decatur, IL. We thought this way we could break it in by the time we got home. The month was January and it was bitter cold, so we threw on some World War II flight suits we had with us. We also had a winter windshield, leg shields and a lap robe. We underestimated how cold and snowy it was. Dad and I took turns on the trike. Even though I was only 13, I knew how to drive the pickup and any motorcycle. I thought to myself, 'This will be really fun!' Two hundred fifty miles didn't seem like a long way. We started on our journey, but soon realized that the rider could only go about 25 miles before he became half frozen and had to stop and switch to driving the truck! It also was only a two-lane road and it was slick with snow and ice. The trip took us all day! Now, many years later, I look back and think this is one of my many exciting experiences I had with my dad." ❋ JD

"If you get to Buddy Stubbs H-D dealership, make sure to see his personal museum, which is awesome. When I was doing a book signing for Buddy some years ago, I stayed at his home. This is before he built his museum. I slept in a room with some antique motorcycles. I remember waking up and smelling oil. Sure enough, the antique bikes in the bedroom were leaking a bit. I laughed, for it brought back lots of fun memories as a kid with my dad. When he saw a little puddle of oil under a bike, he would laugh and say, 'It is just marking its spot!'" ❋ JD

"The Schulteti family has a dealership spanning four generations. I always love going there because there is so much history all in one place." ✳ JD

ABOVE: Bob Schulteti on a 1929 JD motorcycle with a double sidecar at his dealership in Indianapolis, IN. Jean Davidson is in the sidecar.

"I have been invited to lead motorcycle rides for many charitable events, from helping to find a cure for autism to helping with a Headstart program for the Rincon Indian tribe in California. Now that I have my own charity, many organizations have held rides to benefit it. This is helping the Yell and Tell program reach children all over the world and is saving many lives!" ✸ JD

"One of the grade schools I spoke at in Illinois had a wonderful program called 'Hog Wild About Reading.' They used charts that tracked how many books each student had read. For every book a H-D Hog would move up the chart! Being a school teacher, I always love any new way to encourage children to read more. The day I was there, the students dressed up in motorcycle attire and got to sit on a real bike supplied by the local dealer. Even the principal rode his H-D to school that day." ✸ JD

ABOVE: Lakota chief and Jean Davidson in Sturgis, SD.

RIGHT: Welcome sign at a ride for Yell and Tell that was put on by Zylstra Harley-Davidson in Elk River, MN.

The country cottage of Walter Davidson's wife, Emma.

"In 2011, I was over at my great-grandmother Emma Davidson's country house in Menomonee Falls, WI. It was a beautiful spring day, and my mother and I walked the grounds and she reminisced about her memories of visiting there when she was a child. The place was used by Emma as a kind of woman's retreat where she and her friends would go to get out of Milwaukee and relax. They played a lot of cards and had wonderful parties that people in the area still talk about. During our visit we decided to host a motorcycle ride in memory of Emma, and the Country Canter motorcycle event was born." ▨ JDO

"Emma Davidson's country house was donated to the Menomonee Falls Historical Society. My grandmother's home is designated as an official historical site and is now a museum. The house dates back to the Civil War and still has many of the antiques that my grandmother collected on display. It is a great place to visit and what a great place to start an annual ride!" ✸ JD

Jon Davidson Oeflein and his wife, Kristi, leave on the 2012 Country Canter ride.

(Clockwise from above)

Jon's son, Carter, riding around the grounds on his 1972 Harley-Davidson Rapido.

Dave Berndt was one of many riders who participated on the ride in 2012.

Rick Suchon

Mark and Betty Gebler

Andy (on bike), Gail and Jay from Baer H-D

2012 Emma Davidson Country Canter.

"The first annual Emma Davidson Country Canter was a big success. It was held in conjunction with the annual Old Falls Village Days, which draws many visitors who get to see antique tractors, crafts and pioneer demonstrations. I want to thank all the riders who participated, especially everyone from the Badger Heritage Chapter of the Antique Motorcycle Club of America. The weather could not have been better and lots of bikes went on the ride through the Holly Hill area. All bikes are welcome, so hope to see you at the next Country Cantor!" ▨ JDO

"Over the years several historical buildings have been moved to the grounds of my grandmother's estate. These include a train depot, a school house, a farm house and a cabin. They were all open for tours during the event. We also held a silent auction and a 50/50 raffle to benefit Yell and Tell. I want to thank everyone who helped and hope to see you every June as the Country Canter will hopefully grow and grow!" ✻ JD

I Ride.

I ride because the wind calls me.

I ride because the road bends and twists to test me.

I ride because nature wants to show me her treasures.

I ride because the earth begs me to explore.

I ride because I am free to do so.

By John Clark

INDEX

Bruce, Kathy Davidson, 156

Catskill Mountain Endurance and
 Reliability Run, 15, 158–159

Davidson, Alexander, 67, 72–73

Davidson, Alexander Jr., 67

Davidson, Allan, 48–49

Davidson, Arthur, 2, 4, 6–7, 10–11, 13,
 18–22, 26–27, 35, 37, 43, 46, 60, 69, 72,
 74, 77–78, 93

Davidson, Arthur Harley, 4, 27, 35, 37, 69,
 72–73, 79–81, 154

Davidson, Barbara, 69, 83, 88, 104, 113,
 146

Davidson, Bessie, 10

Davidson, Bruce, 71

Davidson, Christine, 83

Davidson, Clara, 27

Davidson, Doris, 53, 56–57, 82–83, 87–88

Davidson, Elizabeth, 10, 78

Davidson, Emma, 42, 90–91, 162, 164, 166

Davidson, George, 78

Davidson, Gordon McLay, 1, 32, 47–59,
 60–61, 68–69, 76, 80–83, 87–88,
 103–104

Davidson, Janet, 10–11, 78

Davidson, Jean, 71, 73, 82–84, 88–89, 92,
 104, 113–114, 118, 121, 144, 149–152,
 154–157, 158–159, 161–163

Davidson, Karen, 118, 156

Davidson, Margaret (McFarlane), 78

Davidson, Margaret (Scott), 10, 67, 72

Davidson, Michael, 118, 156

Davidson, Nancy, 85, 118, 155–156

Davidson, Robert, 47

Davidson, Walter, 1–3, 7–8, 10, 13–18,
 23–26, 31–32, 34–37, 40–43, 45–47, 49,
 61, 64, 69, 70–71, 74, 76–77, 80–81, 86,
 90, 103, 107, 132, 164

Davidson, Walter C., 47–49, 60–63, 68–69,
 76, 92, 139

Davidson, William A., 1–3, 6–7, 11–13,
 18, 32–36, 38–40, 43, 46, 49–50, 55,
 64–66, 74–75, 78

Davidson, William C., 10–11, 13, 18, 32,
 67, 72, 78

Davidson, William H., 65–66

Davidson, Willie G., 66, 85, 89, 92,
 117–118, 155–156

Evinrude, Ole, 4, 78

Forge, Stella, 44

Gettleman, Frederick "Fritzy," 40–41
Goldsmith, Paul, 136

Harley-Davidson
 first factories, 11–12, 23
 hillclimbs, 140–143
 Models
  AMF Roadmaster, 107
  California Sport Glide, 112
  EL, 1, 100
  FL, 114–115, 146–147
  FXR, 111
  Hopeful, 151
  Knucklehead, 101
  M-125, 153
  Model 10B, 23
  Pocket Valve, 130
  Rapido, 165
  Servi-Car, 146, 161
  Silent Gray Fellows, 34
  Super Glide, 100
  Topper scooter, 108
  XLH-1000, 109
  XR-750, 116
 racing, 130–139
 setting up dealerships, 27–30, 92–95
 snowmobiles, 98–99
Harley-Davidson Museum, 125, 155
Harley, John, 64, 154
Harley, Sarah, 34, 64
Harley, William J., 49, 65–66
Harley, William S., 1–2, 5, 7, 11, 13, 16–18,
 24–25, 27, 32–40, 46, 49, 64–66, 74–75,
 77–78, 113
Haydel, Crystal, 45

Knievel, Evel, 116–122
Knuth, Bill, 22, 26, 93, 141

Lang, Carl Herman, 28–29
Lee, Susan Davidson, 100, 154
Leonard, Joe, 134

Macintosh, Keith, 72
Marshall, Charles "Dick," 146–147
McDonell, Heather, 73

McLay, James, 10

Oeflein, Annie, 71
Oeflein, Carter, 100, 113–114, 154, 164
Oeflein, John, 85, 88–89, 92–95, 98,
 105–106, 114, 146–149
Oeflein, Jon Davidson, 70, 85, 93–96, 105,
 107, 110–111, 113–114, 118, 125, 148,
 154, 157–159, 164–165
Oeflein, Kristi, 113, 154, 164
Oeflein, Lori Jean, 70, 93, 96, 112–113,
 118, 148
Oeflein, Max McLay, 71
Oeflein, Nicolas Davidson, 71, 100, 113,
 154
Oeflein, Peter John, 70, 85, 97–98,
 105–106, 114–115, 132, 157
Oeflein, Susan, 70, 96–98, 106, 113
Oeflein, William McLay, 70, 85, 93, 96, 98,
 101, 106, 118, 132, 146
O'Hearn, Sarah Harley, 155

Petrali, Joe, 131

Rayborn, Cal, 138–139
Reiber, Herb, 140

Schulteti, Bob, 162
Sherrit, Maggie, 72–73
Sinclair, Mike, 72
Stocking, Mary Harley, 81, 155
Stubbs, Buddy, 121, 160–161

Harley Family Tree

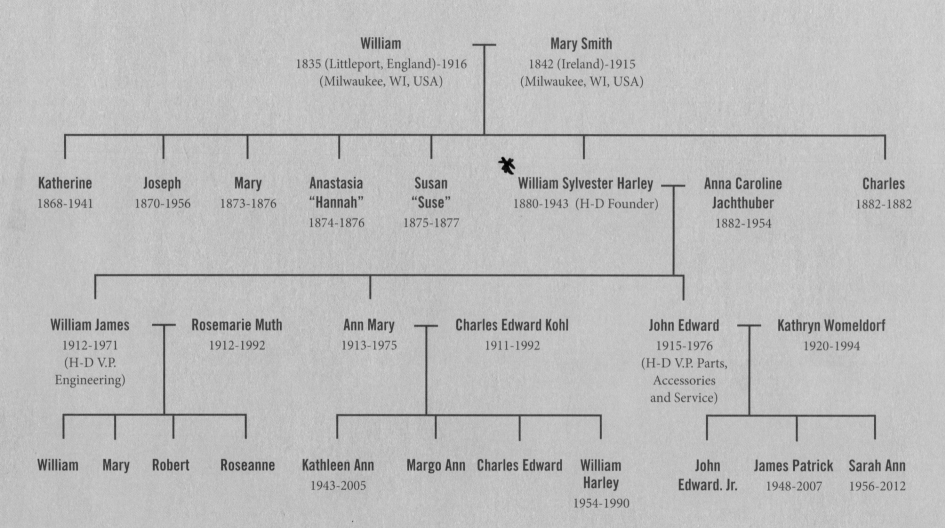

William
1835 (Littleport, England)-1916
(Milwaukee, WI, USA)

Mary Smith
1842 (Ireland)-1915
(Milwaukee, WI, USA)

Katherine
1868-1941

Joseph
1870-1956

Mary
1873-1876

Anastasia "Hannah"
1874-1876

Susan "Suse"
1875-1877

William Sylvester Harley
1880-1943 (H-D Founder)

Anna Caroline Jachthuber
1882-1954

Charles
1882-1882

William James
1912-1971
(H-D V.P. Engineering)

Rosemarie Muth
1912-1992

Ann Mary
1913-1975

Charles Edward Kohl
1911-1992

John Edward
1915-1976
(H-D V.P. Parts, Accessories and Service)

Kathryn Womeldorf
1920-1994

William

Mary

Robert

Roseanne

Kathleen Ann
1943-2005

Margo Ann

Charles Edward

William Harley
1954-1990

John Edward. Jr.

James Patrick
1948-2007

Sarah Ann
1956-2012

Unfortunately, this family tree does not show all the family members.